ROUTLEDGE LIBRARY EDITIONS: AGRICULTURE

Volume 17

TECHNICAL CHANGE, HUMAN CAPITAL, AND SPILLOVERS IN UNITED STATES AGRICULTURE, 1949–1985

TECHNICAL CHANGE, HUMAN CAPITAL, AND SPILLOVERS IN UNITED STATES AGRICULTURE, 1949–1985

KLAUS W. DEININGER

Routledge
Taylor & Francis Group

LONDON AND NEW YORK

First published in 1995 by Garland Publishing, Inc.

This edition first published in 2020
by Routledge
2 Park Square, Milton Park, Abingdon, Oxon OX14 4RN

and by Routledge
52 Vanderbilt Avenue, New York, NY 10017

Routledge is an imprint of the Taylor & Francis Group, an informa business

© 1995 Klaus W. Deininger

British Library Cataloguing in Publication Data
A catalogue record for this book is available from the British Library

ISBN: 978-0-367-24917-5 (Set)
ISBN: 978-0-429-32954-8 (Set) (ebk)
ISBN: 978-0-367-25465-0 (Volume 17) (hbk)
ISBN: 978-0-367-25468-1 (Volume 17) (pbk)
ISBN: 978-0-429-28795-4 (Volume 17) (ebk)

Publisher's Note
The publisher has gone to great lengths to ensure the quality of this reprint but points out that some imperfections in the original copies may be apparent.

Disclaimer
The publisher has made every effort to trace copyright holders and would welcome correspondence from those they have been unable to trace.

TECHNICAL CHANGE, HUMAN CAPITAL, AND SPILLOVERS IN UNITED STATES AGRICULTURE, 1949–1985

KLAUS W. DEININGER

GARLAND PUBLISHING, Inc.
NEW YORK & LONDON / 1995

Library of Congress Cataloging-in-Publication Data

Deininger, Klaus W., 1962–
    Technical change, human capital, and spillovers in United
States agriculture, 1949–1985 / Klaus W. Deininger
        p.   cm. — (Garland studies on industrial productivity)
    Includes bibliographical references and index.
    ISBN 0-8153-2139-2 (alk. paper)
    1. Agriculture—Economic aspects—United States—States—
Statistics. 2. Agricultural innovations—Economic aspects—United
States—States—Statistics. 3. Agriculture—Labor productivity—
United States—States—Statistics. I. Title. II. Series.
HD1769.D45 1995
338.1'0973'09045—dc20   95-31442

Printed on acid-free, 250-year-life paper
Manufactured in the United States of America

Table of Contents

Tables

vii

Figures

Appendix Tables

Preface

Based on a detailed adjustment for the quality of inputs and outputs, this study develops state-level measures for total factor productivity growth in US agriculture which are used to determine (i) the presence and determinants of convergence across states; (ii) the contribution of individual factors of production to productivity growth; (iii) the importance of spillovers across states; (iv) the economic effects of, returns to, and factor biases of research and extension.

A new highly disaggregated data set on production, research, and extension is used to derive state-level estimates of total and partial factor productivity growth for US agriculture in 1949-85 and to identify the contribution of conventional and nonconventional inputs to such productivity growth. Adjustment for quality of human capital, physical capital, and outputs, leads to estimated total factor productivity growth rates that are significantly lower and more uniform across states than those obtained by other studies. Since 1949, rates of total factor productivity growth converged across states. Access to a commonly accessible (spillover) pool of research-induced knowledge was an important determinant of such convergence. Technical change and research were found to be labor- and land-saving and capital- and purchased input-using. A considerable part of productivity growth was embodied in improved inputs.

While rates of return to research investment are still high, there is a marked gap between social and locally appropriable returns, which appears to have widened over the period. Although the numerical values obtained depend on assumptions concerning the impact of research on the knowledge stock in use, the study clearly points towards the high importance of spillovers. Such an importance of spillovers cannot only provide an explanation for the widely observed "underfunding" of research but also has potentially far-reaching implications for the funding of agricultural research systems beyond the US.

This study would have been impossible without the data collected by Phil Pardey and Barbara Craig. It benefited greatly from discussions with Sandra Archibald, Hans Binswanger, Gershon Feder, Terry Roe, Vernon Ruttan, Ed Schuh, and Burt Sundquist. Particular thanks are due to my parents and my wife, Dina Umali-Deininger, whose continuous support helped to shape more than this study.

Technical Change, Human Capital, and Spillovers in United States Agriculture, 1949–1985

I

INTRODUCTION

There are two central issues in studies of productivity growth and the impact of public agricultural research on such growth. One is the measurement of changes in agricultural productivity and the other concerns the link between research and productivity growth. This chapter briefly summarizes these issues, discusses the main hypotheses guiding the investigation, outlines the objectives of the study, and provides an overview of the remaining chapters.

THE ISSUES

There is a broad consensus in the literature that during the post-World War II period productivity in the US agricultural sector increased at an average annual rate of more than one percent, well in excess of the rate of productivity growth in the private, nonfarm economy (Jorgenson and Gollop 1992). But the data on which these inferences are based are wanting in some important respects (Griliches 1963, USDA 1980, Shumway 1985). And despite recent improvements in response to some of the criticisms raised, a number of deficiencies remain (Trueblood and Ruttan 1992). To what extent improved data would lead to a revision of previous total factor productivity (TFP) estimates is unknown. More accurate and detailed data may not only affect our views of productivity developments within US agriculture but may also revise significantly our estimates of various production parameters, including substitution elasticities among inputs, and economic effects such as factor biases of technical change.

1

Public agricultural research is taken to be one of the main sources of productivity growth in US agriculture. A large and influential literature has determined that rates of return to agricultural research were indeed very high (Hayami and Ruttan 1985). This led to the two conclusions that (a) the institutional basis for agricultural research in the US provides an appropriate mix of central and decentralized funding and decision-making, and (b) higher investment in agricultural research is economically justifiable. Rates of return to research in excess of the marginal cost of capital imply there is considerable "underfunding", i.e., a marginal investment in research would yield returns higher than the cost of such capital. Indeed the conclusion drawn from a large number of studies which calculated extraordinarily high returns to agricultural research is that underfunding of US agricultural research is pervasive (Evenson et al. 1987). Estimates of the effects of research are, however, subject to the data shortcomings embodied in the data on which they are based and may, in addition, suffer from omitted variable bias (Pasour and Johnson 1985). Furthermore, the lack of an economically coherent explanation for this phenomenon is unsatisfactory from an economic point of view as it would imply lack of economic rationality in the allocation of capital resources.

HYPOTHESES

With respect to the above issues, the main hypotheses underlying the empirical investigation are as follows:

(a) Failure to systematically account for the changing quality of inputs and outputs has led previous studies to report overly high rates of productivity growth. Our revised estimates of productivity growth, based on disaggregated and quality-adjusted data, are likely to be lower than those obtained in other studies. In line with similar exercises for the whole economy (Jorgenson and Griliches 1972) we expect that although these quality adjustments reduce measured productivity growth, they do not eliminate it. Such adjustments are also expected to attribute a greater role to the phenomena of "embodied" growth and "biased" rather than Hicks-neutral technical change, since adjustment for quality of inputs implies that a greater portion of the observed increase in output is in fact due to input quality enhancements (e.g., improvements in human and physical capital).

(b) We expect that total factor productivity growth rates converge across states, and hypothesize that one of the main reasons for such convergence is states' ability to access a common pool of technology. Such a tendency towards convergence could be counteracted by immobility of certain factors, which might lead individual states to specialize in a direction consistent with their original factor endowment. The relative importance of each of these factors is an empirical issue.

(c) We distinguish, conceptually and empirically, between local (direct) and social (spillover) effects of research. We expect that this will reduce the estimated local (appropriable) return to research and can provide an explanation for the phenomenon of "underinvestment" mentioned above, parallel to the problems encountered in the provision of other public goods. From a social perspective, such "underfunding" may be more severe the greater the difference between social returns to research and the cost of capital; from the state-level administrator's point of view, a socially suboptimal funding level may be more rational the greater the difference between the nonappropriable returns to research (via spillovers) and the appropriable returns (via own research).

(d) We expect research (and extension) to increase output or decrease cost both directly (i.e., in the form of "own" research) and indirectly (in the form of "spillins"). No a priori predictions concerning the magnitude of the social or local return to research can be made.

OBJECTIVES

The above listed hypotheses give rise to the following objectives for this study:

(a) Improved data

- An objective of the research reported herein is to construct a data-set to provide a revised set of estimates on productivity growth in US agriculture at the state level.

- The data-set thus constructed will facilitate a more detailed descriptive characterization of spatial and temporal differences in agricultural production, in particular changes in the level and the composition of outputs and inputs, both conventional and nonconventional.

- Based on comparison of state-level rates of productivity growth, the quantitative effects, and thus the empirical importance of quality adjustment for productivity measurement, will be assessed.

(b) Agricultural growth

- Estimates of productivity change at the state and regional levels will be used to assess the pattern of convergence of state-level growth rates of factor productivity in agriculture over the period 1949-85 and identify any possible reasons for the pattern so assessed.

- Factor biases of productivity growth and substitution elasticities between factors at the aggregate level, as well as for individual regions, will be measured. This can provide evidence to support and/or broaden existing theories of technical change in agriculture such as the induced-innovation hypothesis.

(c) Optimal funding and orientation of agricultural research

- The relative importance of own research (performed within the state) as compared with a common knowledge stock to explain productivity growth and cost of production will be assessed.

- It will be determined whether the public good nature of research can explain some of the empirically observed underfunding of research in a way that can be more readily rationalized from a conventional economic perspective.

- Potential implications of the analysis for the socially optimal amount of research to be undertaken, the distribution of research activities between the local and the public sector, and the mechanisms used to implement desired funding levels, will be used to highlight a number of topics for further research.

The rest of the thesis is structured as follows. In chapter two we describe, in some detail, the construction of the data set. We report on the categories of inputs and outputs included, the procedures used to adjust for variations in input quality, and the methods used to construct the nonconventional input variables. Regional quantity indexes for the conventional input aggregates (i.e., land, labor, capital, and purchased inputs) and for nonconventional inputs (i.e., research and extension) are presented and, as far as possible, compared with input and output trends reported in previous studies.

In chapter three, we discuss estimates of total factor productivity growth obtained from using Divisia index number procedures and from estimating a production function with a time trend, respectively. We use partial and total factor productivity indexes to investigate whether the rate of growth in state-level productivity has converged over time and use the results of the econometric estimation to account for the contribution of individual factors to the measured growth of output.

Chapter four is devoted to an investigation of the economic effects of research and extension using a cost-function framework. We first use the cost function to derive elasticities of factor substitution and to determine the factor bias of productivity change. Incorporation of the research and extension variables then facilitates an assessment of the factor bias effects of local and spillin research and extension. We also report a range of estimates of the marginal productivity of research and consequent internal rate of return to research. We do this using various assumptions about the structure of the lag between research and changes in the stock of knowledge as well as the likely size of the bias due to omitting a private research variable from the model.

II

AGRICULTURAL PRODUCTION, RESEARCH, AND EXTENSION: A QUANTITATIVE DESCRIPTION

This chapter describes the construction and main characteristics of the data that are used to determine development trends of US agriculture in general and the effects of research and extension on agricultural production in particular. In comparison with other studies, two features are noteworthy:

(a) In constructing estimates of the conventional inputs used in US agriculture we have sought to implement, as far as possible, the suggestions of Griliches (1960), AAEA task force (1980), and Shumway (1988) aimed at reducing biases resulting from mismeasurement. It has long been recognized that avoidance of such biases through careful adjustment for changes in quality of inputs and/or outputs, minimization of aggregation bias, and appropriate treatment of durable capital, will all affect the productivity "residual" obtained from conventional growth-accounting exercises. As the necessary disaggregation entails use of data at the state level, these data can be drawn upon to provide a more detailed description and analysis of the development paths of different states and regions, a topic which will be explored in chapter 3.

(b) With regard to nonconventional inputs such as research and extension, we discuss issues of intertemporal as well as interspatial aggregation. While intertemporal aggregation of research expenditures to represent the aggregate knowledge stock has received some attention in the literature, there has been relatively little discussion of issues involved in interspatial aggregation which arise because of the transferability of technology across states. We distinguish between the stock of knowledge generated within any state and the knowledge stock upon which a state can draw as a result of research activities in other states. This distinction will be used in chapter 4 to identify the separate economic contribution of these two sources of new knowledge separately and to outline consequences for research policy that result from the public good character of agricultural research.

CONCEPTUAL BACKGROUND

One of the fundamental aspects of productivity measurement is to distinguish between movements along an isoquant in response to changes in relative factor prices and productivity changes or (inward) shifts of the isoquant. In order for indices of aggregate inputs and aggregate outputs to be useful in analyzing changes in productivity it is necessary that they abstract from price-induced substitution effects to the degree that is possible. Richter (1966) and Hulten (1973) have shown that the Divisia index exhibits an invariance property, i.e., it remains unchanged if changes in the factor mix are due solely to changes in relative prices. This index can be defined for outputs and inputs, respectively, as

$$\dot{X} = \sum_{i=1}^{n} \left[\frac{W_i X_i}{\sum_{i=1}^{n} W_i X_i} \right] \dot{X}_i \tag{1}$$

$$\dot{Q} = \sum_{j=1}^{m} \left(\frac{p_j Q_j}{\sum_{j=1}^{m} p_j Q_j} \right) \dot{Q}_j \tag{2}$$

where m is the number of outputs and n is the number of inputs; p_j denotes the price for the j-th output and w_i the price for the i-th input. In order to make this formula, which requires continuous measurement, operational, one has to use a discrete approximation to equations 1 and 2. We use the Törnqvist-Theil approximation to the Divisia index, defined by

$$\ln\left(\frac{Q_t}{Q_{t-1}}\right) = \frac{1}{2}\sum_{j=1}^{m}(S_{j,t}+S_{j,t-1})\ln\left(\frac{Q_{j,t}}{Q_{j,t-1}}\right) \tag{3}$$

$$\ln\left(\frac{X_t}{X_{t-1}}\right) = \frac{1}{2}\sum_{i=1}^{n}(s_{i,t}+s_{i,t-1})\ln\left(\frac{X_{i,t}}{X_{i,t-1}}\right) \tag{4}$$

where $S_{j,t}$ is the value share of output j in total output and $s_{i,t}$ is the share of factor i in total cost, both at time t. Calculation of an index of inputs and outputs according to equations 3 and 4 is then relatively straightforward, provided the necessary data are available.

DATA MEASUREMENT

US agriculture during the period 1949-85 was characterized by considerable technical change and changes in the mix of inputs. An influential literature has described and analyzed these productivity changes and the contribution of public agricultural research at the aggregate level. Although such analysis has led to valuable insights, the development of individual states within the aggregate has not received detailed attention, primarily due to lack of sufficiently disaggregated data. If such analysis is to be undertaken in any meaningful way, the data must reflect the insights gained from the literature on productivity measurement and quality adjustment. There are three main findings in this literature, namely

(a) To avoid aggregation bias[1] a high level of disaggregation is required.

(b) It is useful for many purposes to measure inputs and outputs in quality-adjusted units[2].

(c) Information provided by markets should be used wherever available[3].

In order to implement these concerns, we use data on labor and land (Pardey and Craig 1991), for capital (Craig, Pardey and Deininger 1993), and for research and extension (Pardey, Eveleens, and Hallaway forthcoming) which in the following will be referred to as the Pardey-Craig-Deininger (PCD) data set. These data incorporate the above measurement concerns in the construction of input and output indexes as follows:

An index of aggregate *output* is constructed using state-level prices-received, quantity, and value data for a total of 49 commodities which are detailed in table 2.1.

Table 2.1:   *Commodities Used in Construction of the Törnqvist-Theil Output Index*

Field Crops	Livestock	Fruits	Vegetables	Other
Barley	Broilers	Apples	Beans	Honey
Corn	Cattle	Apricots	Carrots	Horticulture
Cotton	Eggs	Cherries	Cauliflower	Tobacco
Flax	Hogs	Grapefruit	Celery	
Hay	Milk	Grapes	Cucumbers	
Oats	Sheep	Lemons	Lettuce	
Peanut	(meat)	Oranges	Onions	
Potato	Turkey	Pears	Sweet Corn[a]	
Rice	Wool	Pecans	Tomato	
Rye		Peaches		
Sugarcane		Strawberries		
Soybean				
Sorghum				
Sugarbeet				
Wheat				

[a]   There are two categories (fresh and processed) each for sweet corn and tomatoes.

This set of commodities is more disaggregated than outputs considered in previous studies, with an important difference being the inclusion of separate price- and quantity measures for horticultural produce.[4] Total sales of the 49 output categories used, together with government payments, account for more than 90 percent of gross farm income as reported by USDA.[5] Price and quantity information for the outputs are mainly from *Agricultural Statistics* while data for individual commodities (such as horticultural produce) are from unpublished

USDA data sources. State-specific changes in the relative importance of individual commodities and price differences between states for the same commodity group illustrate the usefulness of such disaggregation. Table A 2.1 in the appendix illustrates that even if commodities are preaggregated into the five groups (field crops, livestock, fruits, vegetables, and other) mentioned above, there were substantial changes in the relative importance of commodity-groups in various states between 1949 and 1985. While the share of crop production increased at the cost of livestock production in mid-western (IL, IN, IA, MI, MN, OH) and some other states (LA, NV, WY), the opposite was true for AZ, AR, NC, and TX. The importance of the "other" output category increased considerably in MA, CT, and RI. A summary of these changes is provided in table 2.2, which gives for each commodity group the states for which a group, in terms of value share in output, was most and least important in 1949 and 1985, respectively. The table illustrates the substantial differences in the importance of field crops, which account for more than 70% of output in some states but for only about 7% in others. In contrast, livestock products made up more than 20% of total output in every state. While FL, CA, AZ, and WA had the highest shares for vegetables and fruits in both periods, the "other" category was characterized by diversification out of tobacco and increased specialization in horticultural produce.

Output prices for individual commodities also varied widely across states. Appendix table A 2.4 illustrates that in 1985 the coefficient of variation for output prices across states, which should equal zero with perfectly integrated markets and in the absence of transport costs, exceeded one for 15 out of 49 commodities, mainly fruits and vegetables. Such price variation may reflect differences in product quality that would influence the decision of profit-maximizing producers concerning the optimal mix of outputs and which would not be captured if average national prices were used to aggregate quantities.

Table 2.2:   *Percentage Share of Commodity Groups in Total Output, Highest and Lowest States, 1949 and 1985.*

	1949		1985	
	Highest	Lowest	Highest	Lowest
Field Crops	70.6 ND	7.1 FL	76.2 IL	7.3 CT
	60.7 AR	11.3 CT	75.0 ND	9.1 RI
	56.9 ID	13.0 RI	71.0 LA	13.1 MA
Livestock	75.1 VT	25.7 FL	79.8 VT	21.0 FL
	74.6 NH	27.5 AZ	72.2 DE	23.6 NJ
	69.5 WI	29.2 ND	65.3 WI	23.2 IL
Fruits	46.3 FL		30.5 FL	
	16.6 CA		20.0 CA	
	14.9 WA		19.0 WA	
Vegetables	13.5 AZ		13.3 CA	
	10.6 CA		12.0 FL	
	8.0 FL		10.8 AZ	
Other	46.5 NC		66.5 RI	
	25.4 SC		38.7 MA	
	21.3 CT		35.2 NJ	

We first calculate an *explicit* quantity index of output using equation 3 and price and quantity information for the 49 commodities listed above. While this index accurately reflects the income derived from marketed outputs, it does not account for income from non-market activities, in particular government payments. The importance of income from non-production, farm-related activities, mainly from government set-aside programs, increased considerably during the 1970s and the 1980s.[6] Appropriate treatment of these programs poses empirical and conceptual difficulties. Given the multitude of government programs and subtle variations in their character (often requiring reduced use of other inputs as well), accurately netting out the inputs used for such programs in any year is difficult. While such programs are likely to affect profit-maximizing farmers' input and production decisions and should thus be included in econometric estimations, it is not clear whether income derived from non-production should be included in index numbers intended to measure changes in productivity.

Given these difficulties, we construct an *implicit* quantity index of output using commodity price and quantity information on the measured outputs, together with an estimate of total farm income that includes non-production income. Denoting total income for time period t by I_t, then, using Fisher's weak factor reversal property (Capalbo and Antle 1988), the following relationship holds;

$$Q_{t+1} \approx \frac{Q_t P_t}{P_{t+1}} \frac{I_{t+1}}{I_t} \tag{5}$$

The assumption required for this procedure to be applicable, i.e., for the implicit index to be unbiased, is that the rate of change in the Divisia price index for measured outputs equals the rate of change in the unobserved price index for non-production income. Empirical computation, using the USDA total income figure,[7] indicates that the difference between these two alternative output indices is not very large (see tables A 2.16 and A 2.17 in the appendix). In the following we will always use the explicit index throughout. While this will lead to a conservative estimate of TFP growth, this bias is not very large.

To construct an aggregate *input index* we distinguish 12 classes of purchased inputs, 32 classes of labor, 3 classes of land, and 10 classes of other capital, all of which are enumerated in table 2.2. Tractors and combines are further differentiated into 21 tractor types and 7 types of combines based on various performance categories. Details of the construction of price and quantity data for each of the above categories are discussed below.

Table 2.3:   *List of Inputs Used in Construction of the Törnqvist-Theil Input Index*[8]

Labor	Land	Capital	Purchased inputs
Operator labor: 30 classes by age-education Hired labor Unpaid family labor	Nonirrigated cropland Irrigated crop- land Range & Pas- ture	*Physical:* Autos Buildings Combines Forage equ't Tractors Trucks *Biological:* Dairy cows Beef cows Sheep Sows	Electricity Feed Fertilizer Fuels and Oils Machine hire Miscellaneous Pesticides Repairs Seed

LABOR

To measure labor in agriculture, and to account for the substantial changes in the mix and quality of agricultural labor in the post World War II era, we constructed measures of hours worked and implicit wage series for each of 32 distinct types of labor within each state. We differentiate between hours worked by hired workers, family members, and 30 classes of farm operators with different age and education profiles. *Census of Agriculture* data on the age characteristics of farm operators was used in conjunction with state-level *Census of Population* data on the number and earnings of rural males in various age-education classes to construct opportunity cost measures of the earnings profiles for farm operators within each state. We also incorporated data from the *Agricultural Census* on days worked off-farm by farm operators to take into account the substantial but uneven shift toward part-time farming. Data from *Farm Labor* were used to measure hours of family labor. An implicit quantity measure of hired labor was derived from ERS data tapes reporting state-level expenses for hired labor. The state specific price for hired and family workers is the wage rate for hired workers reported in *Farm Labor*.

CAPITAL

Durable capital items are not "used up" during one production cycle. To determine the service flow or rental, ρ, from these goods requires making assumptions that enable the expenses associated with the purchase of such assets to be apportioned to individual production periods.[9] Because USDA data on the machinery service flow used in agricultural production are particularly weak,[10] we opted to form our own estimate of the service flow from capital.

The two main considerations in valuing the capital stock are (a) assumptions on the pattern of depreciation, δ, the expected life span, L, and, if data on the age/vintage distribution of the capital stock are not available, on the average age, a, of the capital stock, and (b) the choice of an appropriate interest rate r. Given these parameters, we can use the declining balance method[11] to approximate depreciation of capital and thus the capital service flow used in production at any point in time.

We define a *class* of capital goods as characterized by a common lifespan, L, and an identical rate of depreciation, δ. Quality differences, e.g., due to vintage effects, define different *types* within any class of capital. Referring to the list of capital inputs described in table 2, tractors would be considered a class distinct from, say, combines or autos, while different types of tractors are characterized by their respective vintages and/or horsepower categories.

In order to derive the depreciation and lifespan parameters for numeraire types within each of the different classes of capital we make use, as much as possible, of the information provided by market valuations, based on two principles:

(a) The market value, MV, of any class of capital items is equal to the discounted present value of the (expected) flow of future services, ρ, from a representative or numeraire good in this class[12]. With a given lifespan, L, average age, k, interest rate, r, and a depreciation rate, δ, this leads to a simple formula to implicitly define λ, the discount factor for any class of capital goods (Craig, Pardey, and Deininger 1993):

$$MV\,(L,k,r,\delta) = \frac{\rho}{1-\left(\dfrac{1-\delta}{1+r}\right)^{L-k+1}} = \frac{\rho}{\lambda(L,k,r,\delta)} \qquad (6)$$

(b) Types and/or vintages, T, within any capital class can be transformed into units of the numeraire type N in this class by applying a quality adjustment factor Φ, which can be defined as the ratio of the market values of the type of good in question and the numeraire good in that class.

$$\Phi\,(N,T,L,k,r,\delta) = \frac{MV_T}{MV_N} \qquad (7)$$

The prices for used machinery of different classes as obtained from various machinery dealers' guides and "blue books" were used to derive values for lifespan L, average age a, and depreciation δ, for representative items within each of the capital classes identified for this study. Assumptions concerning the average age of machinery in each class, a, are unavoidable if the service flow is sensitive to variations in the age or vintage of capital items, but more detailed information on the age/vintage structure of the capital stock on farms is not available. Such assumptions were necessary for all types of mechanical capital except tractors and combines for which more detailed data were used. We derived the average age a of the capital stock on farms of every class of capital from the assumed lifespan L of the numeraire item.[13] The parameter values derived for different capital classes, and the resulting parameters using an interest rate r of 4% which can be used in the formulas given above, are summarized in table 2.3.[14]

Table 2.4:   *Parameters Used to Calculate Service Flows for the Capital Stock in US Agriculture*

	L	*a*	*δ*	*λ(L,1,r,δ)*	*λ(L,a,r,δ)*	*(1-δ)ᵃ⁻¹*
Physical:						
Autos	9	4.5	0.2257	0.2748	0.3312	0.35938
Buildings	45	22.5	0.0499	0.0879	0.0987	0.32442
Combines	15	7.5	0.1423	0.1856	0.2230	0.34145
Forage Eqt.	15	7.5	0.1423	0.1856	0.2230	0.34145
Tractors	15	7.5	0.1423	0.1856	0.2230	0.34145
Trucks	10	5	0.2057	0.2533	0.3056	0.35481
Biological:						
Cows	5	2.5	0.3690	0.21598		0.63095
Sheep	6	3	0.3187	0.18342		0.46415
Sows	3	1.5	0.5358	0.34648		0.68129

Note: $\lambda(L,1,r,\delta)$ is the discount factor for new numeraire types of machinery while $\lambda(L,a,r,\delta)$ denotes the discount factor for numeraire types of average age a.

Equipped with this information we used either aggregate figures on the number of units of each capital class on farm, as reported every five years by the *Agricultural Census*, or detailed sales information for individual types of capital, obtained from unpublished farm machinery dealers statistics, to derive service flow and service price estimates for all the durable capital items.

(a) For the nine types of capital goods where aggregate class counts, CC, of the number of items in any capital class, but no information on the distribution of vintages over time, are available, we derived the average age a of the capital stock on farms as half the value of the expected lifespan. Together with the interest rate, r, and the rate of depreciation, δ, this enabled us to express the machinery stock in terms of a numeraire machine. Use of the adjustment factor Φ, and prices of new numeraire items P_t, then facilitates the derivation of the market value of the capital stock in every year according to

$$MV_t = (1-\delta)^{a-1} \cdot \Phi \cdot CC_t \cdot p_t \qquad (8)$$

(b) For tractors and combines, unpublished data on state-level purchases of 21 tractor types by horsepower and combines[15] of eight different types[16] are available from 1964. We denote the value of capital purchased in year t-i by V_i

and use this figure, together with the rate of depreciation δ, to calculate the market value of these two capital classes as

$$MV_t = \sum_{i=0}^{L} V_{t-i} \cdot (1-\delta)^i \qquad (9)$$

Given the market value of capital stocks, the service flow, ρ, used in any year can easily be derived by multiplying the market value by λ, the class-specific discount factor so that

$$\rho = \lambda \cdot MV_t \qquad (10)$$

The information on total value of services from any capital class, as well as the quantity measure implicit in the stock of capital, make it possible to construct service prices or rental rates. This information on prices, implicit quantities, and total value of the service flow for capital in US agriculture can be inserted into equations 3 and 4 to construct a quantity and/or price index of total capital inputs.

LAND

The land input is the service flow from land of three basic types: pasture or rangeland, nonirrigated cropland, and irrigated cropland. Our quantity measure of land differs from the "land in farms" figure commonly used in that our figure excludes non-grazed forest and woodland that is counted as land in farms but not in agriculture. Our measure also includes tracts of federally-owned land that was rented or leased for rangeland grazing purposes. The price weights used in aggregation were annual, state-level cash rents. When missing observations made it necessary, imputed rents were calculated using the correspondence between observed rents and land values. table A 2.5 in the appendix illustrates that in most states the value share of this type of land increased considerably over the study-period. The corresponding price and quantity data indicate, however, that this is due to an increase in the relative price of grassland rather than a significant reduction in the area of irrigated land.

PURCHASED INPUTS

We use expenditures for nine broad classes of purchased inputs. Most of them are implicit Divisia indexes of input aggregates derived from preaggregated value measures that include seed and feed, fuel and oils, elemental fertilizer, repairs, and a "miscellaneous" category that includes insurance, veterinary services, fencing, and so forth.

A descriptive summary of input shares for land, labor, capital, and purchased inputs for the three states with the highest and lowest share of these inputs, respectively, in 1949 and 1985 is provided in table 2.4. There are large differences in output shares across states and these have not narrowed during the study period. Input shares in 1985 ranged from 66% to 3% for land, from 37% to 5% for labor, from 28% to 9% for capital and from 69% to 20% for purchased inputs. Compared with 1949, the data indicate that labor's share has uniformly decreased while the shares of purchased inputs and, to a lesser degree capital, have generally increased over time.

Table 2.5: *Percentage Shares of Land, Labor, Capital, and Purchased Inputs in Total Cost for the Three States with Highest and Lowest Shares for each Input, 1949 and 1985*

	1949				1985			
	Highest		Lowest		Highest		Lowest	
	%		%		%		%	
Land	65.60	NV	2.33	NJ	65.61	NV	3.01	CT
	48.70	UT	4.81	DE	37.51	WY	3.09	RI
	35.27	AZ	4.95	RI	37.12	NM	4.02	NH
Labor	52.81	MS	6.46	NV	37.46	WV	4.97	NV
	51.33	AL	12.44	AZ	33.97	KY	6.32	AZ
	51.30	SC	17.47	UT	33.86	TN	10.52	CA
Capital	21.67	CT	8.72	MS	27.99	WV	9.09	AZ
	19.53	WY	9.36	AR	25.39	NH	9.75	NV
	18.48	SD	9.50	AZ	24.27	CT	10.38	DE
Pur-chased Inputs	59.50	NJ	15.68	NV	68.58	DE	19.67	NV
	52.77	CA	17.17	KY	56.11	CA	27.17	UT
	48.70	MA	17.50	TN	55.47	FL	28.25	WV

OUTPUT AND INPUT TRENDS

The nature of the data can be illustrated using interspatial or intertemporal comparison of indexes and/or value shares of output and input aggregates. At the aggregate level it emerges that, the indexes constructed here are, with some notable and potentially important differences, in accordance with the trends reported by other studies. Disaggregation, however, indicates that national aggregates conceal a large degree of interregional variation. To illustrate temporal and spatial aspects of input and output quantity-indexes we disaggregate national figures using 11 production regions[17] in the text and provide state-level data in the appendix tables.

A summary of the level and growth of the explicit aggregate output index is given in table 2.5. According to our estimates the overall rate of growth of output in US agriculture over the 1949-85 period was 1.58% per annum. Underlying this figure there is considerable regional variation. Output increased by 2.44% annually in the Pacific region, but decreased in the Northeast. States with output growth in excess of 3% annually are FL, GA, AR, DE, AZ, while CA's output grew faster than 2.5% per annum. In contrast, output decreased by more than 0.5% in MA, NH, and NJ. In the aggregate, our figure is slightly higher than the 1.44% obtained by Capalbo and Vo (C&V, 1988) for 1948-83, but substantially lower than the 2.38%, 1.92%, and 1.98% annual growth rates of output, obtained by Huffman and Evenson (1993), Jorgenson and Gollop (1992), and Ball (1985), respectively[18]. This may be due to quality adjustment, i.e.,, the use of state-level prices, and/or the reduction of the residual "other" category.

As noted above, an implicit output quantity index was calculated by inserting the Törnqvist-Theil output price index (P_t, P_{t-1}) and the USDA income figure (I_t, I_{t-1}) which includes nonmarketed outputs, into equation 10. The overall rate of increase of 1.62% of this index (tables A 2.16 and A 2.17) is not too different from the rate of growth of the explicit quantity index.

Table 2.6: Törnqvist-Theil Aggregate Output Quantity Indexes, 1980 = 100

	North East 1	North East 2	Corn Belt	Lake States	N'thern Plains	Appala-chian	South East	Delta	South'n Plains	Moun-tain	Pacific	National
Indexes												
1950	111.27	85.46	61.3	61.03	56.5	77.47	51.04	51.59	56.09	54.27	44.03	61.82
1955	117.09	93.79	68.05	68.44	59.88	80.03	57.35	60.53	54.41	60.78	51.95	67.41
1960	108.99	92.33	74.05	73.18	69.93	81.01	62.7	65.31	68.2	65.82	57.59	72.28
1965	105.26	87.51	77.44	72.95	78.99	82.74	71.39	79.61	71.08	71.25	64.36	76.28
1970	99.94	88.49	83.46	77.29	93.02	87.48	81.73	91.42	79.71	84.23	69.55	83.59
1975	95.95	89.43	86.39	77.44	93.38	95.99	97.73	97.01	94.48	90.55	83.71	89.37
1980	100.39	102.11	105.89	101.14	109.89	105.73	106.7	113.36	108.48	100.22	98.59	105.11
1985	105.9	116.74	104.07	108.55	123.62	112.67	111.01	119.18	108.55	103.3	107.47	110.49
Average Annual Rates of Growth (Percentages)												
1949-55	1.02	1.88	2.11	2.32	1.17	0.65	2.36	3.25	-0.61	2.29	3.36	1.75
1955-60	-1.42	-0.31	1.7	1.35	3.15	0.25	1.8	1.53	4.62	1.61	2.08	1.40
1961-65	-0.69	-1.07	0.9	-0.06	2.47	0.42	2.63	4.04	0.83	1.6	2.25	1.08
1966-70	-1.03	0.23	1.51	1.16	3.32	1.12	2.74	2.81	2.32	3.41	1.56	1.85
1971-75	-0.81	0.21	0.69	0.04	0.08	1.88	3.64	1.19	3.46	1.46	3.77	1.35
1976-80	0.91	2.69	4.15	5.49	3.31	1.95	1.77	3.17	2.8	2.05	3.33	3.30
1981-85	1.08	2.72	-0.35	1.42	2.38	1.28	0.79	1.01	0.01	0.61	1.74	1.00
1949-85	-0.13	0.85	1.44	1.57	2.14	1.02	2.12	2.29	1.8	1.75	2.44	1.58

Note: Here and in all other tables with the same layout, values for each year are three-year centered averages; regional aggregates are share-weighted averages of state-level indices with weights equalling the state's share in output (or the respective input).

Levels and growth rates of the *labor* quantity index are summarized in table 2.6. The use of labor in US agriculture declined at an annual average rate of 2.71 percent since 1949. There was an extraordinarily high decrease of labor input in the Delta states (more than 4 percent annually), the Southeast, and also the North East. By contrast, the reduction of labor quantity was much more modest in the Mountain, Northern Plains, and Pacific States, averaging less than 1.65 percent annually in all three cases. Variation is more pronounced at the state level. Labor quantity decreased by almost five percent in MS by more than four percent in SC and AL, but only by about one percent in FL, MT, and NV.[19] The rate of decline in labor use in US agriculture also varied over time with the largest rate of decline during the study period occurring during 1955-60. The decline has moderated since then, with labor use in the Pacific region actually increasing since 1975.

Table 2.7:   Törnqvist-Theil Aggregate Labor Quantity Indexes, 1980 = 100

	North East 1	North East 2	Corn Belt	Lake States	N'thern Plains	Appala-chian	South East	Delta	South'n Plains	Moun-tain	Pacific	National
Indexes												
1950	377.37	241.25	203.92	197.6	176.5	310.93	420.55	457.74	230.62	176.55	183.93	270.72
1955	264.11	195.23	173.66	168.1	159.27	256.81	313.71	351.21	174.75	152.99	155.26	215.31
1960	195.19	156.59	146.17	143.44	139.58	190.21	209.17	228.52	135.18	130.28	127.79	162.1
1965	150.39	130.3	128.64	125.24	125.85	155.46	155.23	170.52	126.86	117.93	110.94	135.53
1970	109.72	105.11	115.11	105.09	114.4	122.85	117.94	120.18	118.84	105.63	95.36	113.61
1975	96.89	103.58	107.47	103	107.58	109.51	110.88	113.11	105.25	100.04	91.58	105.99
1980	99.98	99.99	100.01	99.98	100	100.03	99.99	100.01	100.02	100	100.05	100.02
1985	99.22	97.95	95.06	97.52	96.83	95.82	95.94	96.66	103.28	102.32	106	97.94
Average Annual Rates of Growth (Percentages)												
1949-55	-6.89	-4.14	-3.16	-3.18	-2.03	-3.75	-5.69	-5.16	-5.4	-2.82	-3.33	-4.48
1955-60	-5.87	-4.32	-3.39	-3.12	-2.61	-5.83	-7.79	-8.24	-5.01	-3.16	-3.82	-5.52
1961-65	-5.08	-3.61	-2.52	-2.68	-2.05	-3.95	-5.79	-5.69	-1.26	-1.97	-2.79	-3.52
1966-70	-6.11	-4.21	-2.2	-3.45	-1.89	-4.6	-5.35	-6.76	-1.3	-2.18	-2.98	-3.47
1971-75	-2.46	-0.29	-1.36	-0.4	-1.22	-2.27	-1.23	-1.2	-2.4	-1.08	-0.81	-1.38
1976-80	0.63	-0.7	-1.43	-0.59	-1.45	-1.8	-2.04	-2.43	-1.01	-0.01	1.79	-1.15
1981-85	-0.15	-0.41	-1.01	-0.5	-0.64	-0.86	-0.83	-0.68	0.64	0.46	1.16	-0.42
1949-85	-3.55	-2.41	-2.04	-1.89	-1.61	-3.13	-3.92	-4.12	-2.15	-1.46	-1.48	-2.71

Our labor quantity index is broadly in line with the estimate provided by C&V of an annual rate of growth of -2.9 percent for operator and family labor. In addition to an assessment of aggregate labor input, however, the detailed wage rate data made available for this study makes it possible to define *human capital* as the difference between the total number of hours worked in agriculture, all valued at national average prices for unskilled labor, and the total wage bill. Based on this definition, it emerges that US agriculture has become much more skill and human capital-intensive over time. This change is illustrated in table 2.7, using the share of human capital in total factor cost over time.

These figures, reflecting shares of human capital in *total* factor cost, indicate that in 1985, at the national level, the cost share of human capital (13%) was almost equal to the cost share of physical and biological capital services (17%). The increasing skill-intensity of US agriculture is illustrated by the increase of human capital's share in total *labor* cost from 18 percent in 1949 to 62 percent in 1985, an increase that was most pronounced in the southern states, where human capital's share of labor cost amounted to only about 5 percent in 1949.

Table 2.8:   Percentage Share of Human Capital in Total Factor Cost, 1949-85

	North East 1	North East 2	Corn Belt	Lake States	N'thern Plains	Appala-chian	South East	Delta	South'n Plains	Moun-tain	Pacific	National
Share												
1950	5.59	5.92	6.47	6.98	6.61	3.09	3.48	3.83	5.23	4.29	5.39	5.09
1955	7.18	7.97	8.10	9.07	8.51	7.09	7.14	7.61	7.22	5.67	6.46	7.29
1960	9.38	10.56	10.46	11.90	10.79	11.38	10.19	10.58	9.45	7.04	7.85	9.74
1965	12.90	14.27	13.46	15.83	13.37	16.90	13.26	13.01	12.57	8.94	9.63	12.87
1970	13.47	14.58	13.84	16.16	13.54	17.03	12.24	11.71	13.00	8.61	9.65	12.86
1975	12.01	13.29	11.56	14.46	11.16	15.83	11.26	11.20	11.02	6.98	7.79	11.29
1980	12.72	12.31	10.26	12.80	9.84	14.45	10.14	10.06	9.99	6.26	7.50	10.48
1985	15.28	14.53	12.87	15.02	11.84	17.95	13.30	12.76	13.57	7.95	9.85	12.99
Average Annual Rates of Growth (Percentages)												
1949-55	5.12	6.11	4.59	5.38	5.18	18.09	15.50	14.70	6.66	5.73	3.68	7.44
1955-60	5.51	5.80	5.25	5.57	4.87	9.92	7.36	6.81	5.55	4.43	3.97	5.96
1961-65	6.58	6.20	5.17	5.88	4.37	8.24	5.41	4.22	5.86	4.89	4.17	5.74
1966-70	0.87	0.42	0.55	0.40	0.26	0.14	-1.58	-2.09	0.67	-0.77	0.04	-0.01
1971-75	-2.27	-1.83	-3.54	-2.19	-3.80	-1.44	-1.66	-0.88	-3.24	-4.10	-4.21	-2.57
1976-80	1.15	-1.51	-2.35	-2.42	-2.49	-1.82	-2.07	-2.13	-1.95	-2.16	-0.75	-1.49
1981-85	3.74	3.37	4.63	3.26	3.78	4.44	5.58	4.87	6.31	4.90	5.61	4.39
1949-85	2.75	2.46	1.87	2.09	1.59	4.87	3.69	3.30	2.61	1.68	1.64	2.56

The quantity index of *land* used in agricultural production was fairly stable over time, and decreased by only 0.2 percent in the aggregate. Clearly, the North East is characterized by the most significant (2.3%) annual reduction in land area whereas land use increased slightly in the Southern, Northern Plains, and Pacific states. The national figures also demonstrate the responsiveness of land to the demand for agricultural produce. In the 1966-70 period, as well as the 1976-80 period, the decline of land use which had been observed for earlier periods was reversed and land use actually increased. In the aggregate, the decrease of land input calculated here is slightly lower than the 0.5 percent figure obtained by C&V. This reflects the possibility that low quality land would be the first to be taken out of production, an aspect of the data that would not be properly captured if state-specific prices were not used.

Table 2.9:   Törnqvist-Theil Aggregate Land Quantity Indexes, 1980 = 100

	North East 1	North East 2	Corn Belt	Lake States	N'thern Plains	Appala-chian	South East	Delta	South'n Plains	Moun-tain	Pacific	National
Indexes												
1950	210.63	144.35	99.1	108.83	93.19	127.43	142.28	99.27	88.36	100.9	95.74	105.23
1955	187.64	135.17	98.25	106.87	93.57	116.59	124.06	92.58	91.47	96.53	97	101.28
1960	157.95	125.94	99.37	105.04	95.08	110.86	111.53	87.92	93.24	96.2	96.49	99.96
1965	128.29	113.42	98.65	103.46	95.38	103.36	101.45	88.89	96.06	98.43	96.62	98.52
1970	105.08	100.29	100.46	98.95	98.4	104.08	102.23	99.44	100.92	98.29	94.5	99.47
1975	99.26	98.87	98.79	97.04	98.5	99.36	99.93	97.51	98.41	97.24	96.38	98.13
1980	100.05	100.03	100	100.01	100.01	100.02	100.03	100.02	100.01	100	100.01	100.01
1985	89.13	93.57	97.14	97.92	99.51	95.53	96.21	96.38	98.03	97.85	98.56	97.69
Average Annual Rates of Growth (Percentages)												
1949-55	-2.28	-1.31	-0.17	-0.36	0.08	-1.76	-2.7	-1.39	0.69	-0.88	0.26	-0.76
1955-60	-3.39	-1.4	0.23	-0.34	0.32	-1	-2.11	-1.03	0.38	-0.07	-0.11	-0.26
1961-65	-4.08	-2.07	-0.15	-0.3	0.06	-1.39	-1.88	0.22	0.6	0.46	0.03	-0.29
1966-70	-3.91	-2.43	0.36	-0.89	0.63	0.14	0.15	2.27	0.99	-0.03	-0.44	0.19
1971-75	-1.13	-0.29	-0.33	-0.39	0.02	-0.92	-0.45	-0.39	-0.5	-0.22	0.39	-0.27
1976-80	0.16	0.23	0.24	0.6	0.3	0.13	0.02	0.51	0.32	0.56	0.74	0.38
1981-85	-2.29	-1.33	-0.58	-0.42	-0.1	-0.91	-0.78	-0.74	-0.4	-0.43	-0.29	-0.47
1949-85	-2.3	-1.16	-0.05	-0.29	0.18	-0.78	-1.05	-0.08	0.28	-0.08	0.08	-0.20

In marked contrast with the post-World War II trend in labor use, the flow of services from both physical and biological capital in US agriculture increased, on average, by 2.22% per annum (table 2.9). Use of capital measured in service flow terms increased rapidly in the Pacific states, followed by the Appalachian, South East, Mountain and Delta states but only slowly in the Northeast and the Northern Plains. Over time, the increase in capital services was highest in 1949-55 and during the 1970s, while capital services decreased in the 1980s. The capital service flow increased by more than double the national average in FL (4.9%) and AZ (4.4%) with increases in excess of 3.5 percent in CA and WA (table A 2.10). By contrast, capital input in CT and RI changed little, increasing by significantly less than one percent per annum. The overall increase in the use of capital reported here is higher than C&V's figures as a consequence of quality adjustment.[20] Comparison between the quantity index of capital service flows used in US agriculture in 1949-85 as obtained by the two studies in figure 2.1 indicates that the difference between the two indexes is particularly large in the years after 1970 when our adjustment for the quality of machinery (which starts from 1964) becomes fully effective.

Figure 2.1:   *Törnqvist-Theil quantity index of capital services used in US agriculture, C&V and our estimate, 1950 = 100)*

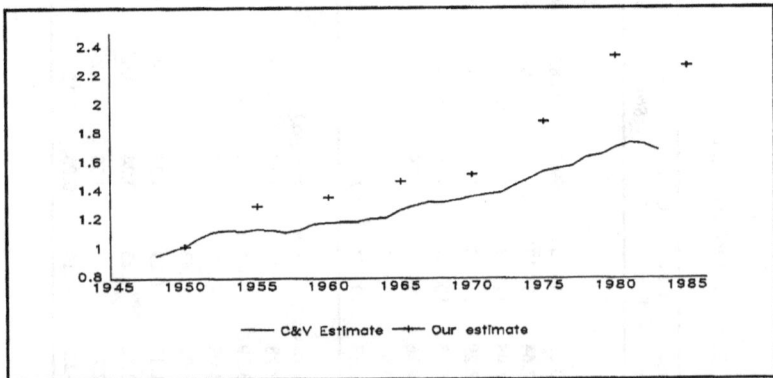

Note: Both indexes have been rebased to 1950=1.0 from 1977 and 1980=1.0, respectively. The C&V figure is for a share-weighted sum of "other capital" (durable equipment and livestock) and structures which, as noted in the main text, are characterized by different growth rates.

Table 2.10: Törnqvist-Theil Aggregate Capital Quantity Indexes, 1980 = 100

	North East 1	North East 2	Corn Belt	Lake States	N'them Plains	Appala- chian	South East	Delta	South'n Plains	Moun- tain	Pacific	National
Indexes												
1950	74.5	53.36	38.66	45.35	49.26	36.55	36.16	37.7	49.42	41.55	30.96	43.27
1955	73.89	62.59	52.96	60.68	66.94	46.52	46.69	53	55.31	51.99	40.76	55.17
1960	70.57	66.72	54.78	66.63	69.04	50.23	50.28	56.99	53.22	54.95	44.76	57.94
1965	63.38	66.21	60.44	68.38	75.18	56.89	54.89	66.76	61.99	60.78	49.5	62.76
1970	62.57	65.21	65.54	65.35	73.94	59.08	61.45	70.13	67.89	62.86	50.24	64.8
1975	76.59	81.67	79.08	76.76	86.29	73.07	80.86	80.37	83.33	76.75	92.75	80.79
1980	99.54	100.13	100.28	101.1	100.53	99.79	100.56	100.81	100.92	99.25	101.61	100.5
1985	118.03	102.57	83.4	94.64	95.89	98.9	94.57	94.4	114.43	105.21	106.37	97.55
Average Annual Rates of Growth (Percentages)												
1949-55	-0.16	3.24	6.5	6	6.32	4.94	5.25	7.05	2.28	4.58	5.65	4.98
1955-60	-0.92	1.29	0.68	1.89	0.62	1.55	1.49	1.46	-0.77	1.11	1.89	0.99
1961-65	-2.12	-0.15	1.98	0.52	1.72	2.52	1.77	3.22	3.1	2.04	2.03	1.61
1966-70	-0.26	-0.3	1.64	-0.9	-0.33	0.76	2.28	0.99	1.84	0.67	0.3	0.64
1971-75	4.13	4.61	3.83	3.27	3.14	4.34	5.65	2.76	4.18	4.08	13.04	4.51
1976-80	5.38	4.16	4.86	5.66	3.1	6.43	4.46	4.64	3.9	5.28	1.84	4.46
1981-85	3.47	0.48	-3.62	-1.31	-0.94	-0.18	-1.22	-1.3	2.54	1.17	0.92	-0.59
1949-85	1.25	1.78	2.1	2.01	1.82	2.73	2.63	2.51	2.3	2.54	3.39	2.22

Use of *purchased inputs*, as shown in table 2.10, increased at an average rate of two percent at the national level. This aggregate figure not only masks the decrease in the Northeastern states but also the significant and fairly wide-spread, shorter run deviations from this longer run trend. Throughout the 1971-75 and 1981-85 periods, there was a substantial decline in the use of purchased inputs in agriculture. The quantity index of purchased inputs decreased by more than one percent annually in NJ and MA. The states with the highest increases in purchased inputs were FL (4.1%), AZ (3.5%), NE (3.3%), NC and AL (3.1%).

Table 2.11:   Törnqvist-Theil Aggregate Quantity Indexes for Purchased Inputs, 1980 = 100

	North East 1	North East 2	Corn Belt	Lake States	N'thern Plains	Appala-chian	South East	Delta	South'n Plains	Moun-tain	Pacific	National
Indexes												
1950	105.99	79.44	41.13	44.08	34.36	43.54	31.37	34.24	34.89	38.27	38.39	45.35
1955	107.04	88.16	50.56	52.68	39.64	51.76	41.25	43.71	38.83	43.17	45.80	52.27
1960	115.99	91.51	60.75	62.84	48.56	62.73	55.98	58.28	51.05	57.92	62.36	62.66
1965	103.30	85.28	69.42	65.11	58.23	69.82	68.01	75.21	63.28	65.37	70.06	69.30
1970	101.39	88.11	84.15	75.93	74.10	81.59	85.90	92.93	81.62	81.78	78.32	82.31
1975	90.17	81.35	85.42	77.66	75.58	77.72	78.80	83.93	77.14	78.50	78.99	80.25
1980	100.11	100.52	100.15	100.91	100.55	100.55	101.48	100.91	101.02	99.83	100.08	100.55
1985	91.84	101.50	94.11	105.08	95.64	97.53	89.06	92.69	84.23	96.21	97.64	95.48
Average Annual Rates of Growth (Percentages)												
1949-55	0.20	2.10	4.21	3.63	2.90	3.52	5.63	5.00	2.16	2.44	3.59	2.88
1955-60	1.62	0.75	3.74	3.59	4.14	3.92	6.30	5.92	5.62	6.05	6.37	3.69
1961-65	-2.29	-1.40	2.70	0.71	3.70	2.16	3.97	5.23	4.39	2.45	2.36	2.03
1966-70	-0.37	0.66	3.92	3.12	4.94	3.16	4.78	4.32	5.22	4.58	2.25	3.50
1971-75	-2.32	-1.58	0.30	0.45	0.40	-0.97	-1.71	-2.02	-1.12	-0.82	0.17	-0.51
1976-80	2.11	4.32	3.23	5.38	5.88	5.29	5.19	3.75	5.54	4.92	4.85	4.61
1981-85	-1.71	0.19	-1.24	0.81	-1.00	-0.61	-2.58	-1.69	-3.57	-0.74	-0.49	-1.03
1949-85	-0.39	0.66	2.26	2.38	2.81	2.20	2.86	2.73	2.41	2.52	2.56	2.03

The above information is summarized in table 2.11 which gives the increase in
aggregate inputs, showing an average annual increase of 0.40%. The regional
pattern described earlier is clearly visible even in the aggregate input figures.
Input use increased at more than triple the national average in the Pacific states
and at more than double that average in the Mountain, Northern Plain and South
East states, but declined in the Northeast, Appalachian and Delta. It is also
instructive to note the distinct spurt in input growth during the latter half of the
1970s. At the state level, overall input showed the largest increases in FL and
AZ followed by WA and CA, and by contrast declined rapidly in NJ, NH, and
WV.

As the national average growth rate of the input quantity index calculated
here (0.40%) is almost identical to the 0.41% derived by Evenson, Landau, and
Ballou (ELB, 1987) it is instructive to compare the differences at the regional
level (refer to the last two rows in table 2.11). Such comparison clearly suggests
that adjustment for quality differences of labor and machinery, while canceling
out in the national aggregate, is of high importance in accurately assessing
productivity growth at the disaggregate level. The rate of input growth suggested
by our figures is lower than the ELB estimate in the Southeast and Delta
regions, presumably due to the fact that our data capture the lower input of
quality-adjusted (unskilled) labor in these states.

Conversely, the rate of input growth calculated here is higher than the one
by ELB in all other regions except for the Mountain states, most likely due to
more accurate accounting for the input of higher amounts of quality-adjusted
(mechanical) capital.[21] The 0.4 percent annual increase in aggregate input
quantity obtained here is also higher than comparable estimates by USDA
(0.06%) and by C&V (0.13%). Based on these higher input quantities, we
would, with equal growth rates of the output index, expect lower growth of total
factor productivity.

Table 2.12:   Törnqvist-Theil Aggregate Input Quantity Indexes, 1980 = 100

	North East 1	North East 2	Corn Belt	Lake States	N'thern Plains	Appalachian	South East	Delta	South'n Plains	Mountain	Pacific	National
Indexes												
1950	139.36	99.48	75.35	79.28	70.27	106.48	94.81	103.31	72.98	69.25	59.39	83.22
1955	127.36	101.39	80.94	84.49	75.5	103.47	90.65	99.94	71.63	71.46	64.51	84.50
1960	121.8	99.45	83.24	87.17	78.52	97.34	85.85	91.88	73.64	77.09	72.50	84.78
1965	104.74	91.48	85.52	85.03	82.19	94.06	84.78	93.58	81.02	81.10	75.92	85.42
1970	94.31	86.87	90.59	83.87	87.46	91.14	89.23	95.37	90.08	87.00	78.11	88.21
1975	89.02	87.2	91.73	86.33	88.44	88.26	87.06	91.14	86.82	86.80	84.89	88.42
1980	99.94	100.27	100.07	100.57	100.28	100.17	100.88	100.54	100.61	99.79	100.22	100.29
1985	97.75	100.15	93.38	100.31	96.74	96.81	91.73	94.24	94.21	98.62	99.64	96.37
Average Annual Rates of Growth (Percentages)												
1949-55	-1.79	0.38	1.44	1.28	1.44	-0.57	-0.89	-0.66	-0.37	0.63	1.67	0.31
1955-60	-0.89	-0.39	0.56	0.63	0.79	-1.21	-1.08	-1.67	0.55	1.53	2.36	0.07
1961-65	-2.97	-1.66	0.54	-0.5	0.92	-0.68	-0.25	0.37	1.93	1.02	0.93	0.15
1966-70	-2.08	-1.03	1.16	-0.27	1.25	-0.63	1.03	0.38	2.14	1.41	0.57	0.64
1971-75	-1.15	0.08	0.25	0.58	0.22	-0.64	-0.49	-0.9	-0.74	-0.05	1.68	0.05
1976-80	2.34	2.83	1.76	3.1	2.54	2.56	2.99	1.98	2.99	2.83	3.38	2.55
1981-85	-0.44	-0.02	-1.38	-0.05	-0.71	-0.68	-1.88	-1.29	-1.31	-0.24	-0.12	-0.79
1949-85	-0.95	0.02	0.58	0.64	0.87	-0.26	-0.09	-0.25	0.69	0.96	1.41	0.40
ELB	-0.63	0.15	0.40	-0.02	0.73	-0.58	0.78	-0.04	0.49	1.04	0.98	0.41

In table 2.13, we summarize the input and output quantity indexes, and the importance of temporal and spatial variation, by providing information on the periods and states with the highest and lowest average annual growth rates of individual inputs and aggregate output in 1949 and 1985, respectively. The marked differences between states in the average annual growth rate of quantity indexes for different inputs and outputs underscores the importance of state-level analysis. Growth of aggregate output over the study period ranged from -0.83% (MA) to 3.40% (FL) per annum. The average annual increase in the quantity of aggregate inputs over the study period ranged from -1.40% (MA) to 2.58% (FL) for the same states, indicating that high increases in observed output quantity are not necessarily associated with increases in productivity, a fact that can be verified from the last row which indicates that indeed FL was characterized by the lowest rate of productivity growth in the whole sample. Average annual growth rates for quantities of individual inputs are widely dispersed as well. They ranged from -4.91% (MS) to -.52% for labor, from -3.11% to 0.44% for land, from 0.78 to 4.89% for capital, and from -1.49% to 4.11% for purchased inputs. The table also points to significant intertemporal differences, indicating that only the quantity indexes of output and labor were characterized by a uniform increase or decrease in all five-year subperiods. The use of land, capital, purchased inputs, and, consequently, the aggregate input quantity index, increased in some periods but decreased in other periods.

Table 2.13:   Summary of Intertemporal and -spatial Variation for Different Output and Input- Quantity Aggregates, 1949-85.

Commodity	TEMPORAL				SPATIAL			
	Lowest growth %	Period	Highest growth %	Period	Lowest growth %	State	Highest growth %	State
Agg. Output	1.00	1981-85	3.30	1976-80	-0.83	MA	3.40	FL
Agg. Input	-0.79	1981-85	2.55	1976-80	-1.40	MA	2.58	FL
Labor	-5.52	1955-60	-0.42	1981-85	-4.91	MS	-0.52	NV
Land	-0.76	1949-55	0.38	1976-80	-3.11	NH	0.44	NV
Capital	-0.59	1981-85	4.98	1949-55	0.78	CT	4.89	FL
Purch. Inputs	-1.03	1981-85	4.61	1976-80	-1.49	NJ	4.11	FL
TFP	*0.75*	*1976-80*	*1.79*	*1981-85*	*0.25*	*FL*	*1.87*	*MS*

RESEARCH AND EXTENSION

The research data used for this study are the newly constructed series of state-level data on research expenditures compiled by Pardey, Eveleens, and Hallaway (forthcoming). This series disaggregates research expenditures into three expenditure classes (land and buildings, instruments, operational expenses and salaries) as well as by source of funding (federal or state). The series extends back to 1890. We use appropriate price indexes[22] to deflate each of these items and, after applying a straight line pattern of depreciation to durable research inputs,[23] compute the total value of the service flows from research in constant 1980 dollars for every year following 1900. Using the faculty salaries index as the relevant price, an implicit quantity index for extension is constructed as well, using the corresponding expenditure data reported in Pardey, Eveleens, and Hallaway. Table 2.14 provides Törnqvist-Theil quantity indices for research service flows. More detailed figures are presented in Appendix table A 2.13 and A 2.12.

During the 1949-85 period, the quantity index for research services increased by 2.85 percent per annum with the highest growth in the Northern Plains (3.56%), Delta (3.21%) and Pacific (3.15%) states. At the state level, growth of research spending was particularly high (above 4 percent annually) in GA, CO, AZ, KS, NC, MS, VA, and NV. The implicit quantity of agricultural research increased most significantly during the 1950s and 1970s with lower overall growth in the 1960s and virtually stagnated with a real decrease in a number of states, in the during the first half of the 1980s.

Table 2.14:   *Törnqvist-Theil Aggregate Research Quantity Indexes, 1980 = 100*

	North East 1	North East 2	Corn Belt	Lake States	N'thern Plains	Appala- chian	South East	Delta	South'n Plains	Moun- tain	Pacific	National
Indexes												
1950	62.63	41.43	44.21	38.6	23.8	30.26	29.29	27.97	37.86	31.94	30.58	36.01
1955	72.48	49.57	50.54	47.01	33.34	37.64	35.24	32.53	46.17	38.67	37.41	43.02
1960	81.57	55.46	57.89	54.7	43.61	44.61	41.74	44.88	53.65	47.38	48.49	51.03
1965	90.36	64.87	66.63	60.08	53.3	53.79	48.87	51.52	51.62	54.44	56.9	58.43
1970	91.57	72.16	78.29	68.97	60.83	58.98	57.46	56.08	60.46	58.82	56.6	64.75
1975	94.5	79.07	82.77	84.13	77.78	74.83	76.94	72.65	81.98	73.91	77.38	78.79
1980	118.66	100.08	102.27	104.58	98.51	99.02	100.4	98.81	100.98	97.33	100.35	100.94
1985	110.61	111.64	104.01	109.58	86.69	99.16	101.36	89.9	122.84	94.75	96.49	101.98
Average Annual Rates of Growth (Percentages)												
1949-55	2.97	3.65	2.71	4.02	6.97	4.46	3.77	3.07	4.05	3.9	4.11	3.62
1955-60	2.39	2.27	2.75	3.08	5.52	3.45	3.44	6.65	3.05	4.14	5.33	3.47
1961-65	2.07	3.18	2.85	1.89	4.09	3.81	3.2	2.8	-0.77	2.82	3.25	2.75
1966-70	0.26	2.15	3.28	2.8	2.68	1.86	3.29	1.71	3.21	1.56	-0.1	2.07
1971-75	0.63	1.85	1.12	4.05	5.04	4.88	6.01	5.31	6.28	4.67	6.45	4.01
1976-80	4.66	4.83	4.32	4.45	4.84	5.76	5.47	6.34	4.26	5.66	5.34	5.08
1981-85	-1.4	2.21	0.34	0.94	-2.52	0.03	0.19	-1.87	4	-0.53	-0.78	0.20
1949-85	1.55	2.72	2.34	2.86	3.56	3.26	3.41	3.21	3.23	2.98	3.15	2.85

The total value of research services in 1985, expressed in constant 1980 dollars, was highest in CA ($ 86 million), followed by NY (53 million), TX (46 million), and FL (44 million) (Appendix table A 2.12). Most of the Corn Belt (IL, IN, IA), the Lake states (WI, MN, MI), and the other Pacific states (OR, WA) spent between 20 and 30 million dollars annually, whereas annual spending on agricultural research was below 10 million dollars annually in all of the Northeast 1 and most of the Mountain states (MT, NV, NM, UT, WY).

For comparative purposes it is useful to augment these measures with a measure of the size of research expenditures in relation to total agricultural production, the so-called research intensity ratio. The research intensity ratios for individual regions, which express research as a percentage of agricultural GDP, are presented in table 2.14. Overall, the research intensity has grown at 4.37 percent annually, from a national average intensity ratio of 0.24 percent in 1950 to 1.19 percent in 1985. Research in relation to agricultural production was highest in the Northeast (above 2%), followed by the Delta states (1.54%). It was fairly low in the Northern Plains (0.51%), the Corn Belt (0.52%), the Lake States (0.75%), and the Southern Plains (0.77%).

Table 2.15: Research Intensity Ratios by Region, 1949-85

	North East 1	North East 2	Corn Belt	Lake States	N'thern Plains	Appala-chian	South East	Delta	South'n Plains	Moun-tain	Pacific	National
Intensity Ratio												
1950	0.45	0.34	0.11	0.16	0.09	0.17	0.45	0.28	0.14	0.21	0.32	0.24
1955	0.72	0.53	0.16	0.26	0.18	0.28	0.51	0.43	0.27	0.37	0.45	0.32
1960	1.06	0.69	0.23	0.36	0.25	0.42	0.63	0.65	0.30	0.51	0.65	0.51
1965	1.42	1.03	0.28	0.47	0.32	0.61	0.78	0.79	0.36	0.73	0.83	0.67
1970	1.92	1.32	0.39	0.60	0.38	0.76	0.97	0.91	0.43	0.76	0.94	0.81
1975	2.03	1.31	0.29	0.56	0.36	0.79	0.93	0.84	0.42	0.78	0.85	0.77
1980	2.67	1.56	0.36	0.56	0.43	0.99	1.08	1.09	0.42	0.95	0.98	0.92
1985	2.49	2.05	0.52	0.75	0.51	1.27	1.38	1.54	0.77	1.23	1.24	1.19
Average Annual Rates of Growth (Percentages)												
1949-55	9.86	9.28	7.78	10.20	14.87	10.49	2.53	8.96	14.04	11.99	7.06	5.92
1955-60	8.04	5.42	7.53	6.72	6.79	8.45	4.32	8.61	2.13	6.63	7.63	9.77
1961-65	6.02	8.34	4.01	5.48	5.06	7.75	4.36	3.98	3.71	7.44	5.01	5.61
1966-70	6.22	5.09	6.85	5.01	3.50	4.50	4.46	2.87	3.62	0.81	2.52	3.87
1971-75	1.12	-0.15	-5.75	-1.34	-1.08	0.78	-0.84	-1.59	-0.47	0.52	-1.99	-1.01
1976-80	5.63	3.55	4.42	-0.02	3.62	4.62	3.04	5.35	0.00	4.02	2.89	3.62
1981-85	-1.39	5.62	7.63	6.01	3.47	5.11	5.02	7.16	12.89	5.30	4.82	5.28
1949-85	4.73	4.98	4.29	4.26	4.80	5.59	3.07	4.72	4.72	4.89	3.73	4.42

The *composition* of research expenditures has changed considerably over time. Figure 2.2 shows the change in the percentage of research funds used for capital expenditures over time for the total US, illustrating that the latter declined to a level significantly below 10%. A similar pattern, though at different points in time, can be discerned for individual regions and/or states as well. This suggests that a certain upfront capital investment has been undertaken by all states in order to provide the necessary research infrastructure.

Figure 2.2:   *Capital i.e., buildings, land and equipment share of total research expenditures, 1890-1985*

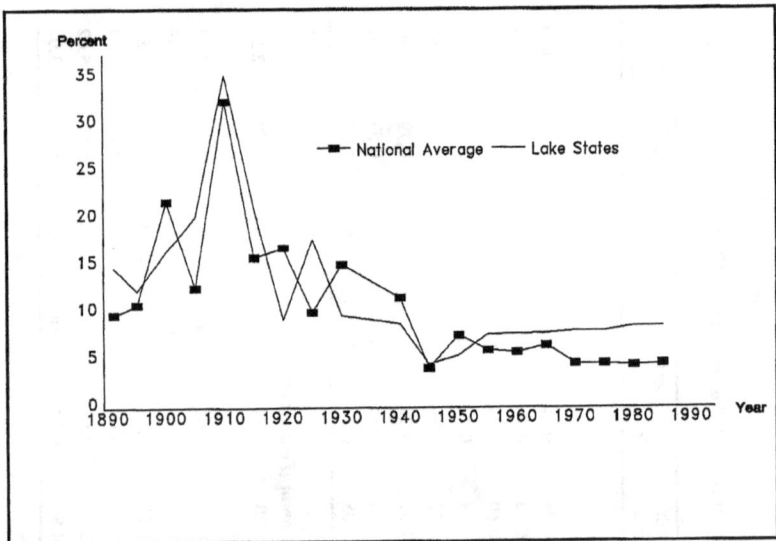

The *source* perhaps more so than the composition of research funds has important implications for the portfolio of research projects being investigated at any point in time. The portion of research funded from federal sources decreased considerably over time, as is illustrated in figure 2.3. The increasing importance of state funds for the financing of research has potential implications for the orientation of the research programs thus supported. State-level decision makers may be more inclined to spend research funds on projects benefiting interest groups within their own state. Furthermore, if they either ignore the existence of positive externalities associated with research or, if recognizing the externalities, act in a self-interested way by equating marginal appropriable returns to marginal costs, underfunding of research activity would result.[24]

Figure 2.3:   *Share of federally sourced funds in total research expenditures, 1895-1985*

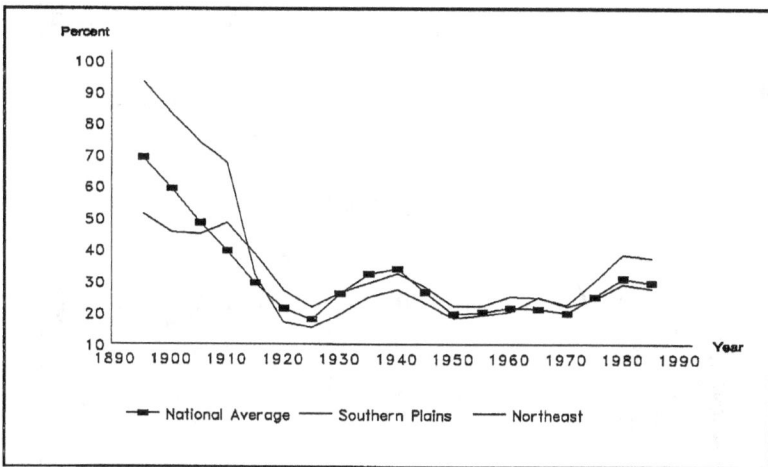

A state-level series on public *extension* expenditures back to 1910 was used to calculate extension intensity ratios. Values from 1949 onward are provided in table 2.16. Extension expenditures averaged 0.84 percent of the value of agricultural production in 1985, reflecting an increase of 3.36 percent annually in real terms since 1949. Very high intensity ratios are observed in the Appalachian, the Southeast, and the Delta regions. The extension ratio is higher than the research ratio in the Corn Belt and the Lake States regions but lower than the research intensity ratio in all other regions. Whether or not this is related to the incidence of private research in any of these areas can not be determined from the available data.

Table 2.16:   Extension Intensity Ratios by Region, 1949–85

	North East 1	North East 2	Corn Belt	Lake States	N'thern Plains	Appala-chian	South East	Delta	South'n Plains	Moun-tain	Pacific	National
Intensity Ratio												
1950	0.40	0.33	0.12	0.15	0.13	0.34	0.35	0.41	0.21	0.22	0.22	0.25
1955	0.58	0.47	0.17	0.24	0.22	0.49	0.43	0.54	0.33	0.32	0.29	0.35
1960	0.81	0.63	0.24	0.33	0.23	0.68	0.54	0.71	0.36	0.39	0.38	0.46
1965	1.06	0.83	0.29	0.40	0.28	0.85	0.64	0.77	0.45	0.49	0.43	0.56
1970	1.59	1.10	0.40	0.53	0.31	1.08	0.81	0.86	0.52	0.51	0.52	0.70
1975	1.72	1.11	0.30	0.49	0.25	1.04	0.72	0.74	0.48	0.46	0.39	0.63
1980	1.89	1.06	0.33	0.47	0.27	1.03	0.82	0.82	0.45	0.47	0.41	0.65
1985	1.96	1.25	0.45	0.52	0.36	1.31	1.03	1.26	0.74	0.71	0.53	0.84
Average Annual Rates of Growth								*(Percentages)*				
49-55	7.71	7.33	7.21	9.86	11.10	7.58	4.20	5.66	9.46	7.78	5.68	6.96
55-60	6.91	6.03	7.14	6.58	0.89	6.77	4.66	5.63	1.76	4.04	5.55	5.62
61-65	5.53	5.67	3.86	3.92	4.01	4.56	3.46	1.64	4.56	4.67	2.50	4.01
66-70	8.45	5.79	6.64	5.79	2.06	4.91	4.82	2.24	2.93	0.80	3.87	4.56
71-75	1.58	0.18	-5.59	-1.56	-4.21	-0.75	-2.33	-2.96	-1.59	-2.04	-5.59	-2.09
76-80	1.90	-0.92	1.92	-0.83	1.55	-0.19	2.64	2.07	-1.28	0.43	1.01	0.63
81-85	0.73	3.35	6.40	2.04	5.92	4.93	4.67	8.97	10.46	8.60	5.27	5.26
49-85	4.39	3.67	3.64	3.42	2.79	3.71	2.96	3.08	3.46	3.22	2.40	3.33

The above description, as well as the analysis presented below, will focus on the role of the public sector. It is, however, important to recognize the contribution made by private research. A comparison of the magnitude of expenditures in each of both systems is provided in table 2.15.

Table 2.17   *Public (USDA and SAES) and Private Agricultural Research Expenditures*

Year	Public Research	Private Research
	millions of 1984 dollars	
1895	30.2	204.8
1900	28.7	
1905	42.8	247.2
1910	94.8	
1915	141.7	347.7
1920	127.3	
1925	291.5	352.1
1930	488.8	
1935	437.8	749.8
1940	523.6	
1945	488.1	471.0
1950	522.5	
1955	623.8	890.6
1960	798.0	1175.3
1965	1068.6	1367.8
1970	1206.3	1486.0
1975	1325.4	1577.8
1980	1585.1	2300.1
1984	1541.8	2444.7

Source: Huffman and Evenson (1993)

Note: Values for 1955 in the private sector and 1895 in the public sector reflect expenditures in the following year (i.e., 1956 and 1896).

These data suggest that private research investment was higher than investment in public research for most of the period under analysis. A comprehensive evaluation of the impact of research must take account of the significant contribution of the private sector, particularly in view of an increasing recognition of the important link between private and public research (Umali 1992). Severe data problems, however, have precluded a more thorough analysis of the role of private research in fostering output or productivity growth in US agriculture.

This omission of private research activity in analyses of the contribution of research to productivity growth has traditionally been justified on the two grounds of its more applied scope, and its concentration on areas characterized by high degree of appropriability:

(a) *More applied scope*: Despite the significant contribution made by private sector research, the areas in which this sector operates are significantly different from the foci of public research activity. Data presented by Huffman and Evenson (1993) suggest that private research is heavily biased towards post-harvest and marketing (52.5%);[25] with activities in the crop sector (24.5%) focussed on disease and pest control (6.6%), plant nutrition (5%), agricultural engineering (6.2%) and breeding in high value crops such as cotton (1.7%), vegetables (1.4%), ornamental (1%), and corn (0.9%). Similarly the relatively low involvement in livestock production (10.5%) focusses on insect and disease control (5.1%) and highly applied breeding.[26] Given its applied character, such private research is unlikely to be a substitute for long-term public research efforts.

(b) *High degree of appropriability*: All of the above areas are characterized by a high degree of appropriability. To the extent that research results are appropriable, and thus reflected in higher input prices, the omission of private research would not bias productivity analysis. If, however, competitive pressure prevents private entrepreneurs from appropriating all the benefits of such research and leads them to pass on some of the productivity gains to producers and/or consumers, private research can yield social benefits that may be of considerable magnitude (Peterson 1976). Some, but not all, of these changes can be captured by making appropriate adjustment for quality changes of inputs (i.e., measuring inputs in units of constant quality as is attempted here). In the ideal case wherein it were possible to fully adjust for input quality changes over time the only unobservable (and thus omitted) component would be "neutral", disembodied advances in technology, such as improvements in management, due to private research.

Despite the potential importance of this topic, empirical studies of the subject are limited and often based on tenuous assumptions in apportioning aggregate private research expenditures to different areas of technology and/or commodities. Using the most comprehensive, but still less than satisfactory, data base on the subject currently available, Huffman and Evenson (1989) come to the conclusion that private firms capture all of the returns to their research activity. Therefore the omission of private research activity does not bias the coefficient on public agricultural research investment in a framework where the latter is included as a nonconventional input.

The consequences for our analysis are as follows:

(a) Wherever interest is in the development of productivity in general rather than the effects of public research, we will use a time trend specification which is not subject to the omitted variable problem noted above.

(b) Lack of data prevents more detailed analysis of private research. Even at the national level, annual data on private research expenditures are available only for the post-1956 period (Huffman and Evenson 1993). Given the paucity of reliable data, the most sophisticated analysis would most probably reflect the assumptions made in interpolating between quinquennial observations for earlier years and, in particular, in apportioning those expenditures to different areas of research. Given the importance of private research and its links with public research effort, more detailed evaluation of the effects of private research is an area where further studies are required.

(c) We note the presence of almost perfect collinearity between aggregate private research and the aggregate (national) value of the spillin variable, the construction of which is explained in more detail below. Regression of aggregate private research on our aggregate spillin variable yields a coefficient of determination of 0.923, and a highly significant coefficient (t-value of 18.6). As this would prevent separate identification of the effects of both phenomena, it is preferable to use the spillin variable, which is available for a longer time period and at a higher level of spatial disaggregation, whenever our interest is specifically in research. We will return later to the issue surrounding the in interpretation of the coefficient on the spillin variable considering the fact that the spillin effects may capture part of the private rather than public research activity.

TEMPORAL AGGREGATION OF RESEARCH

Research affects agricultural production neither directly nor instantaneously. There are time lags between investment in research and the generation of useable technologies, and further lags in the uptake of these technologies. As these new technologies depreciate or become obsolete, their output-enhancing effects eventually wane. With higher levels of productivity, research efforts to maintain the level of productivity become necessary and often consume a substantial share of research spending.[27]

Conceptually (following Griliches 1980), the lagged impact of research on knowledge can be captured by defining K_t, the stock of knowledge available at any point in time as a function of research expenditure, R in current and previous L_R periods.

$$K_t = \sum_{i=0}^{L_R} \lambda_i R_{t-i} + (1 - \delta_K) K_{t-1} \tag{11}$$

where λ_i is the lag operator, R_{t-i} is research expenditure in period t-i, L_R is the lag length, δ_K is the depreciation of knowledge, and K_{t-1} is the knowledge stock in period $t-1$. The nature of this relationship, in particular the shape and length of the research lag is of crucial importance for the rate of return to research.

Empirically, equation 11 is usually implemented by defining the knowledge stock as a weighted aggregate of research expenditures in the previous L_R years where the weights, w_t, specify the shape of the lag profile linking research expenditures in period $t-i$ to the stock of knowledge being used in period t. Information on the average economic lifespan of patents which can be used to make inferences regarding the depreciation of knowledge (δ_K) and thus the weights (w_t) in industry,[28] is generally not available for the agricultural sector, making assessment of the appropriate lag structure difficult. Pardey and Craig (1990) provide evidence that the lag length is considerably longer (at least 30 years) than has been assumed in many of the "first generation" studies of agricultural research, such as Evenson (1967), Knutson and Tweeten (1979), and White and Havlicek (1982). These studies generally assumed a 10-15 year lag with a (symmetric) inverted-V shape. Pardey and Craig's finding is corroborated by Cox and Chavas (1991) who show that a simple inverted V-shaped distribution of research impact appears not to be compatible with data on US agriculture and that there is a significant difference between the lags of private and public research expenditure. In the absence of more detailed information, we use the lag structure by Huffman and Evenson (1989 and 1993) to aggregate research expenditures over time into the state-specific value of the research stock. The sensitivity of the returns to public research investment to variations in the lag structure will be illustrated by comparing results derived using this lag structure to alternative estimates using the lag reported by Cox and Chavas

(1992) below. The shape of these alternate lag-distributions is illustrated in figure 2.4.

Figure 2.4:   *Lag structures of research as used by Huffman and Evenson (1993) and Cox and Chavas (1992)*

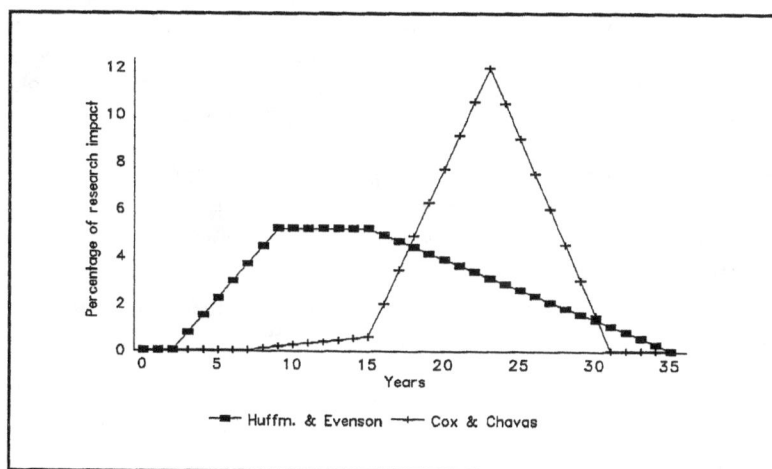

SPATIAL AGGREGATION OF RESEARCH

Knowledge, and its contribution to improvements in technology and allocative efficiency, has long been recognized as a major source of growth (Schultz 1961). The implications of partial transferability of knowledge and the ability to utilize and build on knowledge generated at other places or times, as well as the potential to improve on such knowledge via "learning by doing" are well known (e.g. Arrow 1962). The positive externalities associated with increases in the knowledge stock have recently received renewed interest and more rigorous conceptual treatment in modern theories of "endogenous growth" (e.g., Romer 1986 and 1990, Grossman and Helpman 1991). One of the salient features of the models used in these theories is the existence of positive externalities. These externalities derive from the fact that "knowledge", whether it be embodied or disembodied, possesses certain public good characteristics that can not be (completely) appropriated by the originating firm or individual. This may give rise to increasing returns to scale at the economy-wide level while individual firms' technology is still characterized by constant returns to scale. Such externalities have potentially important theoretical as well as empirical implications.

Conceptually, the public good character of knowledge greatly increases the scope for policy intervention. Barro (1990) showed that with increasing returns to scale at the economy-wide level, government-sponsored investment to increase the economy's knowledge stock can lead to permanently higher growth, despite the deadweight losses associated with the taxation required to fund these public investments. And, if positive externalities exist, market structure and intellectual property rights aspects take on heightened significance with regard to the growth prospects of an economy. Awarding temporary monopoly rights (e.g., patents) will in general increase incentives for private economic actors to engage in research and thus lead to higher rates of growth if positive externalities exist (Grossman and Helpman 1991).

The transferability of agricultural technology, together with the need to adapt such technology to location-specific conditions, have been at the heart of the discussion on the appropriate design of national and global agricultural research systems in order to maximize social benefits (Ruttan 1987 and 1989, Schuh 1976). In our context, two consequences are of particular relevance:

(a) The need to adapt techniques to location-specific conditions, together with the dynamic character of environment-technology interactions that often lead to the deterioration of individual techniques (such as new varieties, pest control regimes, and so on) over time implies that the ability to transfer technology is contingent on an adequate investment in the human and physical infrastructure necessary to adapt, disseminate, and maintain such technology. "Convergence" or "catching up" of individual states in terms of their levels of productivity, due, in part, to their ability to share in a common pool of knowledge, would be expected only if such infrastructure is established and continues to be well-maintained.

(b) Transferability of research, together with scarcity of resources, would provide a strong incentive for individual states to "free-ride" and rely on the technology generated by others rather than contribute to the common technology pool themselves.[29] This would give rise to the typical problems associated with the provision of public goods. If the amount of research provided is based on maximization of the appropriable "local" (state-specific) rather than "social" benefits from this activity, the aggregate amount of research provided would be below the socially optimal level. Certain funding mechanisms, e.g., some kind of co-financing scheme that manages to address the free-rider problem, might give rise to higher social benefits in situations where such a problem is of importance.

A number of studies have undertaken to demonstrate the quantitative importance of spillovers in broadly defined industries as well as agriculture in particular. Aggregate studies of various industrial sectors such as Bernstein (1989) find that the social rate of return to research was between 2.5 and 4 times the private rate of return, depending on the characteristics of the industry. Bernstein and Nadiri (1988) found that across different industries, private rates of return to research were very similar (between 15% and 20%), but that social returns were higher than private returns to research by between 10 percent and 10 times, depending on the industry. Spillover effects remain a significant source of social benefits even if, in a dynamic model, the disincentive to invest in research through the "free-rider effect" is explicitly taken into account. Bernstein and Nadiri (1989) obtain an estimate for the overall social rate of return to research that is between 30% and 123% higher than the private rate of return using such a dynamic model. Jaffee (1986 and 1989) also finds a significant excess of social over private returns from research.

In agriculture, recognition of the potential importance of spillin effects had its origins in the failure to find a significant coefficient for in-state research in regression analysis aimed at finding the sources of state-specific productivity improvement (Latimer and Paarlberg 1965). A number of studies, including Evenson and Kislev (1974), White and Havliceck (1980), Garren and White (1985), and Evenson (1989), suggest that "borrowed" research is an important determinant of productivity growth in agriculture. But there is no consensus on how to measure the "spillover pool" of research and the empirical evidence concerning the quantitative importance of spillovers is mixed. For these reasons we address this issue in some detail in this study.

Conceptually, following Spence (1984), the commodity specific spillin received by any state i (in commodity j) can be represented by

$$S_i^j = \gamma^j (K_i^j) \, \theta^j \, \bar{K}_i^j \qquad (12)$$

where K_i^j is the knowledge stock available in state i, θ^j is the coefficient of transferability for commodity j, $\bar{K}_i^j$ is a summary measure of the research stock in other geographical areas applicable to state i (i.e., the potential spillin-pool), and γ^j is a commodity-specific increasing and concave function. While intuitively appealing, it is difficult to determine observable equivalents for most of these variables.

These difficulties can be illustrated by Huffman and Evenson (1993), who treat the issue in great detail. They a priori restrict the potential spillin pool to states in the same agroecological region, thus excluding the potential for spillins in commodities and/or less applied research areas that are less dependent on the agroecological conditions. They then set θ equal to 1.0 for livestock and to 0.5 for crops. Based on the assumption that γ depends on the research "foci" (i.e., the orientation of research towards either basic or more applied topics) and the agroecological diversity of any state, they also introduced indicators for both these aspects into their "decomposition" regression to determine the effects of research.

While ingenuous in considering a wide range of factors, the particular assumptions on commodity specific transferability appear to conflict with some of the available evidence[30] so we therefore choose not to impose any a priori restrictions in this respect. Rather than base the calculation of an aggregate spillin pool of knowledge on the physical distance between states, we opted to calculate the distance between (or similarity of) states in terms of input-output space. To do so we used a method that was first applied by Jaffee (1986) to characterize firms' position in "technology" space. We assume that the transferability of technology between any two states depends on the "similarity" of outputs produced and inputs used rather than spatial proximity as follows. Given an m-dimensional vector of outputs and an n-dimensional input vector, characterize the "position" of a state in input-output space by a vector $F_i = (F^I$ ... F^m, F^{m+1} ... $F^{m+n})$ where each of the elements F^k denotes the quantity of output or input k. Define a measure of proximity, P_{ij}, between any two states i and j in input-output space[31] as

$$P_{ij} = \frac{F_i F_j'}{\sqrt{(F_i F_i') \ (F_j F_j')}} \qquad (13)$$

For any two states i and j, P_{ij} equals one if both input and output quantities, up to a factor of proportionality, are identical. P_{ij} will approach zero the more dissimilar are the input and output mix between these states.

Calculation of P_{ij}s for the 48 contiguous states in each of the 37 years in our sample indicates a high degree of temporal stability of the P_{ij}'s[32]. On this basis we felt justified in using an average figure for every state over the 1949-85 period in order to construct a [48*48] matrix of "spillin coefficients" P_{ij} (part of which is presented in Appendix table A 3.8). We use this matrix to aggregate research performed by other states into a "spillin pool" S_i which denotes the stock of knowledge generated by other states (j) which is potentially applicable in state i. Formally, S_i is given by

$$S_i = \sum_{j \neq i}^{48} P_{ij} K_j \qquad (14)$$

where K_j denotes the stock of knowledge available in any state j which in our case is approximated by the weighted sum of local research expenditures. Implicitly we assume that the lag structure on own research and the aggregate spillin pool are identical. This assumption can be defended given the lack of proper investigations into the subject which would force basing any other conjectures on ad-hoc assumptions.

Evaluation of equation 14 for every state allows us to classify states into "net receivers" and "net providers" of technology, depending on a comparison of their percentage contribution to total national research expenditures and their share of the spillin-pool. It emerges that CA, FL, NY, NC, and TX (in this sequence) make the most significant net contributions to the spillin-pool while WV, NH, VT as well as UT, NV, and NM derive the highest net benefits from the spillin pool (see Table A 2.14).

Notes:

1. Available data on inputs often necessitates using quantity, price, or value measures that involve some degree of preaggregation. Using such data to form price and quantity indexes yields unbiased indexes only if the rates of growth of the prices or quantities of the items within each preaggregated group are identical. Otherwise there will be aggregation bias leading to distorted estimates of aggregate growth. For example, if rates of change of higher quality inputs exceed the rates of change of lower quality inputs within the same group, then the rate of growth of the group is biased downward relative to an index treating high and low quality items as separate commodities.

2. Griliches (1960) was the first to provide a detailed discussion of the need for appropriate deflators and to illustrate quantitatively the magnitude of errors introduced due to lack of quality-adjustment in some commonly used data for the agricultural sector. The potential magnitude of biases due to quality mismeasurement is also shown in Jorgenson and Griliches (1967 and 1972), and Pardey and Craig (1990).

3. Use of market information is of particular importance to account for quality differences between different vintages of durable capital and different types of output, two areas that will be discussed in some detail below.

4. As can be seen in Table A 2.1 in the appendix, in 1985 horticultural produce accounted for more than one third of total agricultural marketings in northeastern states such as CT, MA, and NJ. Other studies, such as Huffman & Evenson (H&E 1993) apparently include horticultural produce in the "other" category and use a price index for aggregate crop production to derive implicit quantity-measures. This would lead to bias if changes in relative prices for horticultural produce differ from changes in prices for aggregate crop output.

5. The USDA gross farm income figure overestimates total income from production as it includes a number of income streams that are not attributable to production of agricultural commodities (see below). Thus the 90 percent coverage is likely to be a lower bound.

6. In 1985, government payments averaged 4.6% of total farm marketings across all states with a maximum of 18% in Montana. The contribution of government payments to farm income was much lower in 1960.

7. The figure used for "total income" here is defined as the sum of farm marketings, government payments, changes in farmer-owned inventories, and home consumption. In contrast to USDA, we exclude the "other farm related income" category, due to three reasons: (a) a number of the elements included in USDA's "other" category are either not an output from agricultural production (such as income from custom work and machine hire) or can not directly related to agricultural production (e.g. dividend income of farmers); (b) some of the outputs (such as horticulture) which USDA sub-

sumes under "other" are already included in our figure of total farm marketings, thus adding them in would amount to double-counting; (c) the definition of "other farm related income" is not consistent over time. As more income sources (such as income from recreational activities) are included over time, the resulting figure would bias growth of income upward and lead to exaggerated estimates of productivity growth.

8. For a brief summary of data and sources used for each of these categories see appendix table A 2.3.

9. Note that maintenance expenditures are accounted for as a separate input category (repairs).

10. Griliches (1960) indicates that, already in 1957, the value of the machinery stock used by USDA, based on a machinery stock survey from 1949, underestimated the machinery stock by as much as 75%. With minor modifications, this machinery survey still forms the basis of USDA estimates (Trueblood and Ruttan 1992).

11. According to the declining balance method δ_t equals $2/L_t$, where L_t is the mean service life of the asset. As shown by Jorgenson & Griliches (1967) this method is appropriate if the efficiency of capital declines geometrically. Furthermore, straight line depreciation can be understood as a special case of the declining balance method (Craig, Pardey, and Deininger 1993).

12. Implicit in this assumption is the abstraction from market or informational imperfections.

13. The average age a depends only on the probability of survival if there are no pronounced vintage-effects (i.e., extraordinarily high or low rates of new purchases at different points in time). If the rate of capital purchases were constant over time and if the survival probability equaled one, a would be half the lifespan of L.

14. Our choice of an interest rate of 4% is based on the notion (Griliches 1960), that the interest rate used has to be higher than the real rate for government bonds (or corporate stock) which are associated with less risk. As real interest rates for the latter averaged about 2% per annum (Ibbotson Associates 1991), we choose 4% as the applicable real interest rate. This differs from existing studies in that we assume the interest rate to be constant over time and we do not use an "internal" interest rate derived from national account estimates as a residual measure. Jorgenson and Griliches (1972) and Ball (1985) calculate an internal interest rate as a residual return on capital employed in individual sectors using national accounts data. The imputed rates of return on capital fluctuate considerably and pose a number of problems, particularly if only the agricultural sector is considered. Implicit interest rates fluctuated between 4-10% in the household sector, 9-20% in the non-corporate sector, and 6-15% in the corporate sector for the 1950-62 period (Jorgenson and Griliches 1972). Changes in asset prices lead to (implausible) negative interest rates for some years if only the agricultural sector was considered and necessitated the use of

(unspecified) ARIMA procedures to substitute "expected" rather than actual prices into procedures Ball (1985) used to calculate capital service flows.

15. We use census-data, figures on national horsepower-averages, and the average position of states with respect to the national average to backcast these figures for the pre-1964 period.

16. Combine classes are defined by a weighted combination of performance characteristics that include engine capacity (in horsepower), drum width and diameter, shaker area, sieve area, concave area, and tank volume.

17. These production regions are defined as follows: North East 1: CT, ME, MA, NH, RI, VT; North East 2: DE, MD, NJ, NY, PA; Corn Belt: IL, IN, IA, MO, OH; Lake States: MI, MN, WI; Northern Plains: KS, NE, ND, SD; Appalachia: KY, NC, TN, VA, WV; South East: AL, FL, GA, SC; Delta: AR, LA, MS; Southern Plains: OK, TX; Mountain: AZ, CO, ID, MT, NV, NM, UT, WY; Pacific: CA, OR, WA. State-level data in the appendix tables are all arranged according to these production regions.

18. Note that the Huffman and Evenson's data extend until 1982, Ball's data run from 1947 to 1978, Capalbo and Antle's series is from 1947 to 1983, and Jorgenson and Gollop use data from 1947 until 1985.

19. Results for some of the western states may be biased where *nonagricultural* rural wages may have measurable effect on the rural wages which are used here to determine the opportunity cost of *agricultural* labor.

20. C&V obtain a growth rates of 3.1% for structures and of 1.0% for biological capital and durable equipment.

21. This comparison excludes the Northeast where, due to ELB's omission of a number of states, data coverage is not identical.

22. These indexes are an index for faculty salaries which is used to deflate labor and operational expenses; the state and local goods and services index which is used to deflate plant and equipment; and the Handy-Whitman public building cost index which is used to deflate the "land and buildings" component.

23. The assumed average life spans are 10 years for plant and equipment and 50 years for buildings.

24. The same argument applies to individual states in relation to all other producers of the same commodity in the world market (see, e.g., Alston and Freebairn 1988). Note also that central allocation of research funds is potentially associated with monitoring problems concerning the prudent use of federal funds, an issue which could be used in favor of a combination of state and federal funding.

25. This and all following percentage figures refer to total private research expenditures.

26. The breakdown of private research investment by area reported by Huffman and Evenson (1993) is for 1961, apparently the latest year for which such information was available.

27. Plucknett and Smith (1986) indicate that about half of the research spent on US experiment stations is for maintenance.

28. Goto & Suzuki (1989) determine industry-specific rates of depreciation based on the "life span" of technology. Pakes and Schankerman (1984) and Bosworth (1978) specify a net profit maximization model that compares the cost of keeping a patent to the expected profit-earning potential of the patent in order to empirically determine the parameter (δ) for the depreciation of research. Similar considerations led Bernstein (1988) to use a 10% straight line depreciation and Griliches (1986) to use a declining balance (exponential) depreciation of 15% annually.

29. Existence of this problem with regard to agricultural research has been recognized for some time (Latimer and Paarlberg 1965).

30. While greater transferability of research results in livestock as compared with crops is intuitively appealing as far as direct production is concerned, the opposite may be the case with respect to more basic research (e.g., plant breeding and genetic manipulation) which appears to be much easier transferable across plants than across animal species. Indeed, one study (Garren and White 1985) finds evidence of higher spillovers in crops than in livestock.

31. Use of the distance-measure discussed above in industrial studies was based on the position of firms as measured by the output from research activity, in most cases appropriately classified patent data. While use of such a measure (i.e., counts of publications -or their citations- by agricultural experiment stations classified by area of technology) would be preferable to the output-measure used here, the necessary data are not readily available. Our use of the position in input-output space to measure closeness in technology-space would be unbiased if there were perfect congruence between the contribution of a commodity to agricultural product and the research expenditures devoted to this commodity.

32. The coefficient of variation ranges from 0.09 for MN to 0.24 for AZ, DE, and RI and averages 0.14 over all states.

III

PRODUCTIVITY GROWTH IN US AGRICULTURE

In this chapter we apply index number theory to calculate indexes of total factor productivity (TFP) at the state level. We also compare the figures thus derived to estimates of total factor productivity reported by other studies. Our TFP estimates are then used to determine whether productivity growth in agricultural sectors of different states converged over time. An aggregate production function is then estimated to provide a measure of productivity growth and facilitate counterfactual growth accounting.

Three main results emerge from this analysis, namely

(a) The estimated rate of productivity growth is substantially lower than in comparable studies as more of the increases in output are attributed to higher input quality.

(b) State-level differences in partial factor productivities persist but total factor productivities converge across states.

(c) Using the results from econometric analysis to determine the contribution of individual factors of production to productivity growth confirms the results of our index number analysis and indicates the importance of technical change that is "embodied" in human capital and purchased inputs.

CALCULATION OF INDEX NUMBERS

METHODOLOGY

Aggregate total factor productivity (TFP) can be defined as

$$TFP = \frac{Q}{X} \tag{15}$$

where Q represents aggregate output and X represents aggregate input. The change in total factor productivity is then given by

$$T\dot{F}P = \dot{Q} - \dot{X} \tag{16}$$

For small changes in a variable, Z, proportionate rates of change (i.e., dZ_t/Z_t) are approximately equal to logarithmic differences ($\ln Z_t - \ln Z_{t-1}$), thus we can use a discrete approximation to equation 16

$$T\dot{F}P = \ln\left(\frac{TFP_t}{TFP_{t-1}}\right) = \ln\left(\frac{Q_t}{Q_{t-1}}\right) - \ln\left(\frac{X_t}{X_{t-1}}\right) \tag{17}$$

Calculation of an index of inputs and outputs according to equations 3 and 4 above facilitates derivation of a measure of the index of total factor productivity growth in agriculture for each of the 48 contiguous states in the US using equation 17.

Under constant returns to scale, perfect competition, and Hicks neutrality, the same measure can be derived from the primal production function or the dual cost function. Let the production function be defined as $Q = F(X, \tau)$ where Q is a m-vector of outputs, X is a n-vector of inputs and τ is an index of technology, commonly but not necessarily equated with time. Define the primal rate of technological change by logarithmically differentiating the production function

$$\frac{\partial \ln F}{\partial \tau} = \frac{d\ln Q}{d\tau} - \frac{1}{F} \sum_{i=1}^{n} \frac{F_i dX_i}{d\tau} \qquad (18)$$

where F_i is the derivative of F with respect to input X_i. Assuming profit maximizing producers, so that the price of outputs equals the marginal cost of producing them and inputs are paid the value of their marginal product, we can define the primal rate of technological change, $\partial \ln F/\partial \tau$ as

$$\frac{\partial \ln F}{\partial \tau} = \frac{d\ln Q}{d\tau} - \left(\frac{\partial \ln C}{\partial \ln Q}\right)^{-1} \sum_{i=1}^{n} S_i \frac{d\ln X_i}{d\tau} \qquad (19)$$

where S_i is the ith factor's share of total cost, and $\partial \ln C/\partial \ln Q$ is the elasticity of cost with respect to output, which can be used to classify returns to scale. It can be shown (Capalbo and Antle 1988) that a dual measure of technical change as derived from the corresponding cost function $C\ (Q,\ W,\ \tau)$ is equal to the primal rate for constant returns to scale (i.e., $\partial \ln C/\partial \ln Q = 1.0$). Thus, under the maintained assumptions of constant returns to scale, profit maximization, and Hicks neutrality, both index numbers and econometric estimation of a production or a cost function should lead to identical results in assessing the rate of total factor productivity growth.

RESULTS

Over the period 1949-85, total factor productivity in US agriculture --calculated by substituting equations 3 and 4 in equation 17 above and using an explicit quantity index-- increased at an average annual rate of 0.79 percent. This figure increased to 0.83 percent per annum with the inclusion of additional farm-related income from non-production activities, if the implicit rather than the explicit output quantity index along the lines of equation 5 was used. A comparison of aggregate growth rates to the national level studies by Capalbo and Vo (C&V 1988), Ball (1985), Jorgenson and Gollop (1992), as well as the regional study by Evenson, Landau, and Ballou (ELB 1987), which underlie the estimates reported in Huffman and Evenson (H&E 1993), is provided in table 3.1.

Table 3.1:   *Growth Rates of TFP as Calculated by Different Studies*

Time Period	Huffman & Evenson ('93)	Ball ('85)	Capalbo & Antle ('88)	Jorgenson Gollop ('92)	Our Estimate ('93)
1949-55	2.04	2.56	1.18	1.37	0.65
1955-60	2.46	2.75	1.19	2.33	0.79
				1.35	
1961-65	2.66	2.54	1.16	0.63	0.62
1966-70	1.18	-0.07	0.42	1.19	0.79
1971-75	1.53	2.83	2.69	-0.67	0.90
1976-80	0.66	(1.52)	1.21	2.06	0.60
1981-85	(2.13)		(-0.71)	3.58	1.48
1949-85	*1.84*	*1.86*	*1.34*	*1.58*	*0.79*

Note: The periods for which growth of factor productivity is reported by Jorgenson and Gollop are 1947-53, 1953-57, 1957-60, 1966-66, 1966-69, 1969-73, 1973-79, and 1979-85. Coverage is until 1982 for H&E, 1948-78 for Ball, and 1948-83 for C&A. Growth rates which cover only part of the period indicated are enclosed in brackets.

The rate of productivity growth reported here is considerably lower than the rates reported by other studies. A graphical illustration of the evolution of the aggregate index of total factor productivity over time as compared to other studies is provided in figure 3.1.

Figure 3.1:   *Alternative TFP estimates*

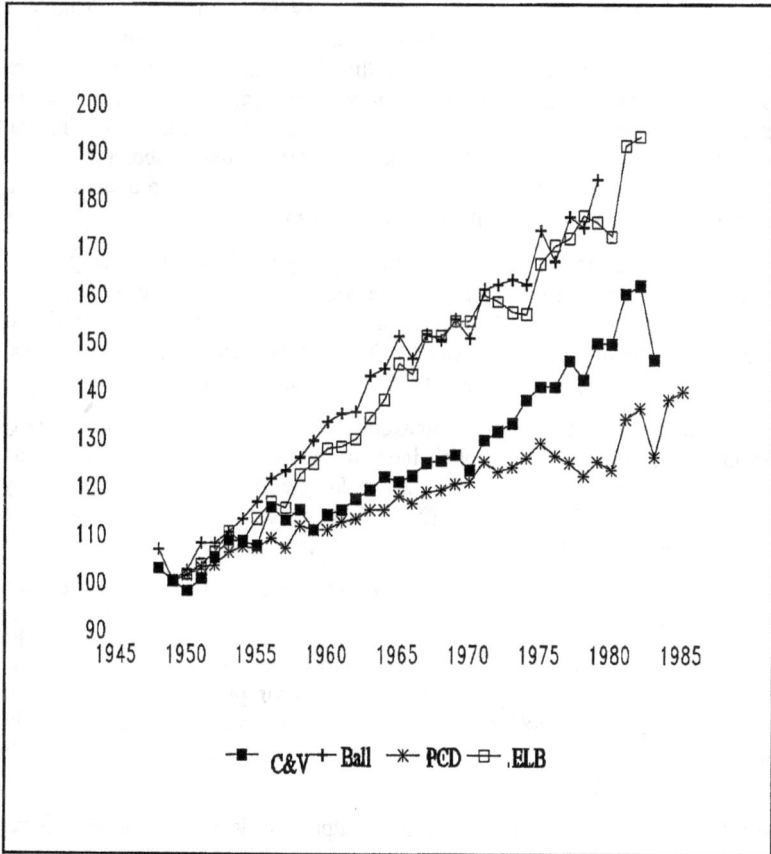

Note: Ball's and C&V's figures are national indexes whereas the national
           aggregate used for H&E figures consists of a simple average across
           states. To facilitate clarity of exposition all indexes were rescaled (not
           rebased) to 1949 = 100.

At a very general level, these two main characteristics can be discerned:

(a) There is a marked difference between C&V/PCD on the one hand and H&E/Ball on the other hand, a difference that persists throughout the period. One potential reason for this result is that C&V and our data make more elaborate attempts to adjust for labor quality[1], thus a large part of the differences can probably be taken to reflect improvements in labor quality (or "human capital"). As the earlier studies did not adjust for improved labor quality, the increase of productivity from such quality improvement ended up in the residual measure rather than being attributed to human capital.

(b) Our estimates of the level of productivity begin to fall considerably below those obtained by C&V after 1970. The respective indices of capital used in agriculture (recall figure 2.1) diverge markedly in the post-1970 period and suggest that the difference in measured TFP can be attributed to more refined adjustment for changes in the quality of capital undertaken in this study.

A regional and time-wise breakdown of our total factor productivity estimate (obtained using an explicit index of the rate of growth in output), and a comparison to the aggregate growth rate for the 1950-82 period reported by ELB,[2] is provided in table 3.2. The underlying state-level data are given in Appendix table A 3.4.

This evidence from the disaggregated state-level data leads to three main conclusions:

(a) There exist considerable differences across regions in measured rates of productivity growth. Average growth of total factor productivity in the Delta region during the 1949-85 period was more than three times higher than the average rate of growth in the Mountain region. This finding is consistent with the results by ELB.

(b) Quality adjustment for inputs and outputs leads to considerably lower estimates of productivity growth in all regions. In comparison to the estimates by ELB and H&E, our estimates are uniformly lower in every region. And, most significantly, the differences are not uniformly spread across the states. The difference is largest in the Pacific and Lake State regions (with their estimate four and three times as large as ours, respectively) and lowest in the Mountain region (with their estimate approximately double ours).

Table 3.2: Regional Rates of Total Factor Productivity Growth, our Estimates by Time Periods and Overall ELB Estimate, 1949-85 (1949=100)

	North East 1	North East 2	Corn Belt	Lake States	N'thern Plains	Appalachian	South East	Delta	South'n Plains	Mountain	Pacific	National
Levels of Total Factor Productivity												
1950	108.19	103.87	98.20	99.14	102.73	100.28	101.67	98.28	89.58	99.93	99.7	99.41
1955	124.79	110.00	99.29	101.55	100.22	105.97	110.02	110.47	89.01	103.46	102.27	102.68
1960	121.63	110.67	102.82	103.45	108.74	113.24	117.54	122.43	100.94	102.53	99.22	106.81
1965	134.78	114.13	104.20	105.30	113.50	118.64	126.34	134.00	96.58	103.82	102.37	110.15
1970	138.41	119.95	105.31	110.92	123.04	126.31	130.87	143.13	96.36	108.43	105.13	114.58
1975	140.04	121.50	107.41	108.89	121.93	138.03	147.96	151.77	114.23	115.80	113.43	119.84
1980	132.06	121.13	118.94	118.58	127.26	135.29	140.02	158.55	114.57	112.67	112.73	123.46
1985	139.04	135.37	123.74	126.23	144.26	145.82	152.73	170.78	120.68	117.40	122.01	132.89
Average Annual Rates of Growth (Percentages)												
1949-55	2.90	1.15	0.22	0.48	-0.49	1.11	1.59	2.37	-0.13	0.70	0.51	0.65
1955-60	-0.51	0.12	0.70	0.37	1.64	1.34	1.33	2.08	2.55	-0.18	-0.6	0.79
1961-65	2.07	0.62	0.27	0.36	0.86	0.94	1.45	1.82	-0.88	0.25	0.63	0.62
1966-70	0.53	1.00	0.21	1.04	1.63	1.26	0.71	1.33	-0.05	0.87	0.53	0.79
1971-75	0.23	0.26	0.39	-0.37	-0.18	1.79	2.48	1.18	3.46	1.32	1.53	0.90
1976-80	-1.17	-0.06	2.06	1.72	0.86	-0.40	-1.10	0.88	0.06	-0.55	-0.12	0.60
1981-85	1.04	2.25	0.79	1.26	2.54	1.51	1.75	1.50	1.04	0.83	1.59	1.48
1949-85	0.68	0.72	0.63	0.66	0.92	1.02	1.11	1.50	0.81	0.44	0.55	0.79
H&E	1.24	1.24	1.47	1.77	1.68	2.49	2.43	3.22	1.70	0.89	1.55	
ELB	1.55	1.55	1.57	1.99	2.09	2.48	2.17	3.12	1.89	1.19	2.04	1.97

(c) Once quality adjustment is made, the rates of productivity growth across states are more uniform than estimates in which such adjustments are not undertaken. The coefficient of variation of the estimated growth rates across states is 0.173 for our figures, as compared with 0.266 for ELB's estimates. The fact that our estimates are not only lower, but also more uniform across states not only suggests that accounting for quality improvements is important, but also points towards the importance of a common pool of knowledge in understanding cross-state patterns of growth, a notion to which we return in more detail below.

The above discussion provides an indication for the existence of differences between ELB's and our results but it does not indicate the significance of such differences. In order to determine whether the annual rates of change and/or the average growth rates suggested by two indices, I and I^*, are statistically significantly different from each other, Craig and Pardey (1990) suggest to perform a regression of the type $\ln I = \alpha + \beta \ln I^*$. If the growth rates suggested by the pair of indices are identical, the coefficients α and β should not be significantly different from zero and one, respectively. In order to determine the significance of deviations between ELB's and our figures, we ran the above regression for each of the 42 states for which ELB provide results over the 1949-82 period, setting I equal to the TFP index obtained by ELB and letting I^* equal our TFP growth rate. With 34 observations for each state, the critical values for the two-tailed t-test are 2.042 (5% level) and 2.750 (1% level). The test statistic for the null-hypothesis that $\beta = 1.0$ follows an F (1,31) distribution with critical values of about 4.16 (5% level) and 7.56 (1% level).

The test statistics provided in table 3.2a indicate that for most states the two estimates are statistically significant at the 1% level. The exceptions are FL, NV, and WA where the differences are not statistically significant and NY, WV, and TX where the differences are significant at the 5% level only. Inspection of the estimated slope coefficients, β, indicates that in 37 of the 39 statistically significant cases, ELB's estimate overstates the growth rate of total factor productivity by 50% (in 29 cases) and by 100% (in 13 cases).

Table 3.2a: *A Statistical Comparison of Our State Level Total Factor Productivity Estimates with those of ELB*

State	Our Est.[a]	H & E[a]	T-statistic:α ≠ 0	F-test: β ≠ 1
Connecticut	131.3			
Maine	157.4			
Massachusetts	144.7			
New Hampshire	151.7			
Rhode Island	206.5			
Vermont	113.6			
Delaware	150.6	227.5	-5.38	32.31
Maryland	132.5	181.7	-5.85	36.54
New Jersey	107.4	136.6	4.74	21.14
New York	128.1	133.6	-2.64	7.25
Pennsylvania	128.5	202.9	-7.30	57.14
Illinois	128.5	165.9	-4.28	20.89
Indiana	126.9	187.2	-6.61	46.92
Iowa	116.4	148.9	-3.68	14.92
Missouri	120.3	184.4	-6.67	48.99
Ohio	123.6	182.3	-5.74	35.42
Michigan	133.8	220.3	-12.64	171.20
Minnesota	128.2	194.0	-7.07	54.34
Wisconsin	116.0	164.8	-5.60	32.58
Kansas	134.7	212.3	-8.20	75.98
Nebraska	133.6	202.2	-7.57	62.89
N. Dakota	160.1	237.9	-4.17	20.81
S. Dakota	140.1	187.4	-4.39	21.97
Kentucky	146.4	224.5	-7.88	66.72
N. Carolina	154.4	263.2	-11.20	145.67
Tennessee	154.5	208.3	-9.58	101.86
Virginia	131.3	186.3	-3.46	13.42
W. Virginia	135.7	186.3	-2.21	5.11
Alabama	177.1	288.6	-15.54	283.67
Florida	106.9	127.5	-0.20	0.06
Georgia	173.3	277.3	-8.62	88.04
S. Carolina	184.0	249.3	-7.14	59.87
Arkansas	159.3	284.0	-11.70	157.01
Louisiana	158.2	217.5	-15.72	271.14
Mississippi	205.9	340.1	-11.59	165.24
Oklahoma	132.5	207.8	-7.34	59.67
Texas	120.3	158.3	-2.19	6.61
Arizona	101.4	100.7	1.54	2.27
Colorado	106.3	162.9	-4.72	23.91
Idaho	130.3	162.9	-12.34	159.18
Montana	140.1	173.0	-3.96	19.08
Nevada	121.7	101.2	0.08	0.72
New Mexico	113.5	141.9	-3.06	10.16
Utah	128.8	115.4	3.39	12.86
Wyoming	121.3	130.3	14.60	194.35
California	117.3	186.2	-5.01	26.82
Oregon	121.2	199.5	-10.93	126.12
Washington	111.3	231.8	0.89	0.59

CONVERGENCE

The question of whether countries with initially low levels of labor productivity can achieve more rapid growth than countries with relatively high levels of productivity has received renewed and considerable interest of late (Baumol 1986 and 1988 and deLong 1988). The state-level data compiled for this study can provide some evidence on this issue while abstracting from the many data measurement and availability problems that come with using international data sets to address this issue. Though our data set is limited to a 37 year period following the Second World War, states began the period with large differences in labor productivity. An additional advantage of using state level US data rather than cross-country data is that differences in the policy environment, the significance of which is debated in a number of recent studies (see, e.g., Backus et al. 1992 and Barro 1991), are less of a problem. Furthermore, rather than using per capita which is a labor productivity measure that may be a very poor proxy for changes in overall productivity, we can make direct use of our data on total factor productivity.

We first calculate indexes of partial factor productivity for different inputs in each state which are summarized in table 3.3. Two observations from this table are particularly noteworthy:

(a) With perfect mobility of factors, partial productivities for each of the inputs should be equalized, leading to a coefficient of variation of zero. Deviations of this coefficient for individual input categories from zero can be used as an index of factor mobility and/or market integration. The persistence of cross-state variation in the partial factor productivities for land and labor suggests that markets for these or other inputs are imperfectly integrated. By comparison, markets for purchased inputs and capital appear more fully, but still not perfectly, integrated.

(b) Over time, the coefficient of variation for land and capital increased. This indicates that some states, at least, which were initially characterized by very extensive (intensive) use of land (or capital) specialized in the direction of their "comparative advantage" and became more extensive (intensive) in their use of the respective factor over time.[3] Conversely, the spatial variation in partial productivities of labor and purchased inputs decreased over the period.

Table 3.3:   *Partial Productivity Indexes of Land, Labor, Capital, and Purchased Inputs, US, 1949 and 1985*

	Partial Productivity			
	Land	Labor	Capital	Pur. Inpt.
Average Level 1949[a]	100	100	100	100
Average Level 1985	265	488	84	92
Average annual growth 49-85	2.67	4.38	-0.47	-0.23
Coefficient of Variation 1949[b]	1.00	0.61	0.38	0.25
Coefficient of Variation 1985	1.15	0.54	0.42	0.22

[a] Partial factor productivity is calculated as output per unit of input, both measured in terms of constant 1980 dollars using the Divisia price indexes constructed for this study as deflators. To illustrate movements over time, the average level for 1949 was normalized to 100.

[b] The coefficient of variation is calculated, in any year, for the level of partial factor productivity across the 48 states included in our analysis.

In total, neither the aggregate values nor the underlying detailed figures point to anything like an equalization of partial productivities across states. The common characteristic in these state-level data is not the equalization of partial factor productivities but rather the growth of land and labor productivity. In fact, there is no state where partial productivities for either labor or land declined over the study period. By contrast, partial productivities for capital and purchased inputs were characterized by a slight decline.

Average rates of growth of total factor productivity in 1949-85, and the 1949-level of labor productivity, are compared graphically in figure 3.2. With the exception that we use a total rather than partial factor productivity measure, this parallels the analysis performed by Baumol (1988).

Figure 3.2:   *Average rate of growth in total factor productivity 1944-85*
               against level of labor productivity in 1949, 48 contiguous US
               states

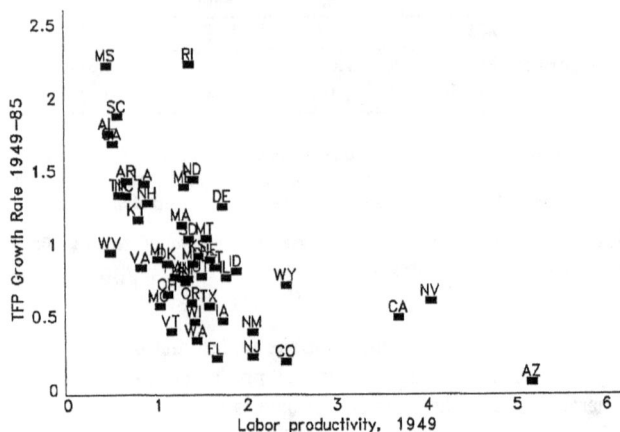

Inspection of figure 3.2 suggests the presence of a negative relationship between the two variables. This negative relationship is confirmed by (a) linear regression of TFP growth rates on initial levels of labor productivity, which yields a significant coefficient of -1.019 (t = -4.72). Thus our data support the notion of a in agricultural productivities across states. However, the R^2 is only 0.32 (compared with 0.88 in Baumol's regression of the rate of per capita output growth on initial labor productivity for an international sample), implying that the level of labor productivity in the initial period "explains" about one-third of the observed differences of the TFP growth rate across states. States with a low initial labor productivity appears to have the potential to "catch up" with other states, presumably by adapting techniques that are already available, but this factor alone is far from sufficient to explain cross-state differences in the growth of total factor productivity. CA and NV, although characterized by high levels of labor productivity, had annual TFP growth rates that were about 0.5%, higher than FL, CO, NJ, NM, WA, WI, IA, or even TX, all states that were characterized by much lower initial labor productivity. Other factors, such as research and extension investments, will have to be investigated to account for these observed differences in productivity growth.

It has long been hypothesized that the public good nature of technical progress is the main factor facilitating "catch-up" (Dowrick and Nguyen 1989). Lack of data, however, prevented an empirical test of this hypothesis in previous studies. The results of such a test, in the form of a regression of TFP growth rates for individual states on changes in a number of conventional and nonconventional inputs and the initial level of labor productivity, for our sample are reported in table 3.4.

Table 3.4: *Regressions of Changes in Total Factor Productivity Growth (1949-85) on Changes in Conventional and Nonconventional Inputs and Initial Labor Productivity.*

	Regr. 1	Regr. 2	Regr. 3	Regr. 4
Intercept			-7.908	-4.99
			(-2.75)	(2.237)
Labor productivity in 1949	-1.019		-0.2835	
	(-4.72)		(-4.31)	
Change in labor quantity		-0.3274		-0.30134
		(-6.76)		(-6.17)
Change in capital quantity				-0.1756
				(-2.22)
Change in purchased input quantity			-0.2120	
			(-3.01)	
Changes in research stock			0.1660	0.11126
			(2.35)	(2.34)
Changes in spillin-stock			2.0447	1.16467
			(3.14)	(2.28)
R^2 (adj)	0.32	0.49	0.48	0.60

Comparison of regressions 1 and 2 indicates that, for the agricultural sector, reduction of employment alone has, for the study period, affected productivity growth in a statistically more significant way (R^2 of almost 0.5) than the initial level of labor productivity. However, productivity growth in conjunction with a reduction in the amount of (measured) inputs is possible only in the presence of improved technology.[4]

Regressions 3 and 4 indicate that, in line with the results by Kim and Lau (1992), a rapid growth of the capital stock tends to be associated with low productivity growth[5]. But, changes in research and the common pool of knowledge were unequivocally associated with higher growth of productivity. It is of particular interest to observe that in both regressions the coefficient on the growth of the spillin-stock is higher than the coefficient on the locally produced knowledge stock by an order of magnitude of almost ten. Increases in the stock of common knowledge seem to have made a quantitatively more important contribution to productivity growth than research investments by individual states.

The evidence provided by indexes of total and partial factor productivity can be summarized in three points:

Embodiment of technical change: Quality adjustment for inputs and outputs apparently reduces, but does not eliminate, measured growth in total factor productivity. This is due to the fact that a greater percentage of the growth in output is attributed to increased "real" quantities of inputs, thus leaving less for the unexplained "residual". Part of what had previously been attributed to technical change may thus in fact reflect use of higher quality inputs, in particular human capital. This implies that part of factor productivity growth would be "embodied" in inputs, and points to the need to investigate neutral as well as biased sources of technical change and to study in more detail the sources of such quality increases, i.e., factors contributing to formation of human capital and increased quality of purchased inputs.

Regional differences: There does not exist a uniform pattern of convergence and/or divergence of partial factor productivities. While partial productivity indexes for labor and land grew in all states, states appeared to specialize, based on their initial factor endowment, in extensive or intensive uses of land and capital. Indexes of total factor productivity, however, indicate there was indeed "convergence" across states in this regard.

Common effects: More uniform rates of factor productivity growth than those obtained by other studies suggest that more disaggregated measurement of inputs and outputs affects resulting estimates of productivity growth. This result also points towards the importance of a "common pool" of technology or the existence of positive externalities which can not be fully captured by the originating state in the generation of technology. Investigation of the factors determining convergence confirmed this conjecture and indicated that, while changes in own research and in the spillin-pool both contribute significantly to productivity growth, changes in the common knowledge stock are quantitatively more important.

ECONOMETRIC ASSESSMENT

THEORY

We take the aggregate production function to be of the form $Q = F (X, T) = F (L, A, P, F)$, where X denotes inputs, T is time, L denotes labor, A land, F capital, and P purchased inputs. Using a translog production function we estimate

$$
\begin{aligned}
\ln Q \,(L_i, A_i, X_i, t) = &\sum_{i=1}^{47} \delta_i D_i + \\
& a_L (\ln L_i) + a_A (\ln A_i) + a_P (\ln P_i) + a_F (\ln F_i) + a_t T + \\
b_{LL} (\ln L_i)(\ln L_i) + b_{LA} &(\ln L_i)(\ln A_i) + b_{LP} (\ln L_i)(\ln P_i) + b_{LF} (\ln L_i)(\ln F_i) + b_{Lt} (\ln L_i) T + \\
& b_{AA} (\ln A_i)(\ln a_i) + b_{AP} (\ln A_i)(\ln P_i) + b_{AF} (\ln A_i)(\ln F_i) + b_{At} (\ln A_i) T \\
& b_{PP} (\ln P_i)(\ln P_i) + b_{PP} (\ln P_i)(\ln F_i) + b_{Pt} (\ln P_i) T + \\
& b_{FF} (\ln F_i)(\ln F_i) + b_{Ft} (\ln F_i) T + \\
& b_{tt} T^2
\end{aligned} \quad (20)
$$

where productivity growth is approximated by an autonomous time-trend (T and T^2) and state-dummies are represented by D_i. Taking the partial derivative of ln Q ( ) with respect to the four factors of production (L, A, P, F) and assuming profit maximization so that each input is paid its marginal product, the share equations for each of the conventional inputs can be written as

$$
\begin{aligned}
S_L &= a_L + b_{LL} (\ln L_i) + b_{LA} (\ln A_i) + b_{LP} (\ln P_i) + b_{LF} (\ln F_i) + b_{Lt} T \\
S_A &= a_A + b_{AL} (\ln L_i) + b_{AA} (\ln A_i) + b_{AP} (\ln P_i) + b_{AF} (\ln F_i) + b_{At} T \quad (21) \\
S_P &= a_P + b_{PL} (\ln L_i) + b_{PA} (\ln A_i) + b_{PP} (\ln P_i) + b_{PF} (\ln F_i) + b_{Pt} T \\
S_F &= a_F + b_{FL} (\ln L_i) + b_{FA} (\ln A_i) + b_{FP} (\ln P_i) + b_{FF} (\ln F_i) + b_{Ft} T
\end{aligned}
$$

Using the definition of growth in total factor productivity from equation 15 above, one can derive the following expression (see Capalbo and Antle 1988 for a detailed derivation) to calculate the rate of productivity growth:

$$T\dot{F}P = \left[\left(\frac{\partial \ln C}{\partial \ln Q}\right)^{-1} - 1\right]\dot{X} + b_t + b_{tt}T + \sum b_{it}\ln X_i \qquad (22)$$

Note in particular, that this specification does not require the assumption of neutral technical change. Furthermore, the use of a simple time trend does not imply any a priori assumptions regarding the origin or nature of technical change; in particular, it captures productivity change originating in part from research performed by the private as well as the public sector. Under the assumption of constant returns to scale, equation 21 simplifies to

$$T\dot{F}P = \sum_i b_{it}(\ln X_i) + b_t + b_{tt}T \qquad (23)$$

and the primal rate of productivity growth thus obtained should be directly comparable with the estimate obtained earlier using an index number approach.[6]

Under constant returns to scale and profit maximization by producers, the coefficients in the share equations are identical to the coefficients of the production function. If deviations from profit maximization are due only to random errors, error terms for each equation are independently and identically distributed and cross-equation correlations are constant. As the share equations are linear in parameters, we can use GLS (iterated seemingly unrelated regression) methods to obtain estimates for the parameters.

Almost perfect collinearity between human and physical capital, as well as purchased inputs (see the correlation matrix in Appendix table A 3.6) would imply low significance of the coefficients on these two variables, if included jointly into the regression. But we did estimate an alternative specification that included unskilled labor, human capital, purchased inputs, and fixed inputs (land and capital) separately as dependent variables in order to demonstrate the effects of human capital. The results for this specification are given in appendix table A 3.5.

RESULTS

After imposing homogeneity and profit maximization restrictions which were not rejected given the data, the coefficients in table 3.5 were obtained.[7]

Table 3.5:   *Coefficients of the Production Function with Time Trend*

Variable	Estimate	Std.Err.	t-value
Intercept	-12.697	0.180	-70.660
Labor	0.166	0.004	43.878
Land	0.276	0.002	130.723
P.Inputs	0.306	0.002	141.220
Capital	0.252	0.004	65.329
Time	0.108	0.003	36.899
Time^2	-0.0002	0.000	-9.050
Labor x Labor	0.020	0.001	20.485
Labor x Land	-0.042	0.001	-63.264
Labor x P.Inputs	-0.005	0.001	-4.698
Labor x Capital	0.027	0.001	27.482
Labor x Time	-0.010	0.000	-45.672
Land x Land	0.071	0.001	73.975
Land x P.Inputs	-0.023	0.001	-29.100
Land x Capital	-0.006	0.000	-13.892
Land x Time	-0.002	0.000	-19.063
P.Inputs x P.Inputs	0.047	0.001	45.959
P.Inputs x Capital	-0.020	0.001	-24.248
P.Inputs x Time	0.003	0.000	33.658
Capital x Capital	-0.001	0.001	-1.054
Capital x Time	0.001	0.000	26.520

The production function estimated using the whole sample is monotonically increasing in conventional factors at the geometric means for the whole sample, for all years, and individual states. Output elasticities for individual factors, evaluated at geometric means for the whole sample, are uniformly positive. Even with the parameter values from national estimates, there are large differences in output elasticities across time and states.[8]   Estimation of the production function for individual production regions, results of which are given in table 3.6, supports the hypothesis that output elasticities for individual factors in various regions were very different from each other.

Table 3.6: *Output Elasticities of Individual Factors as Estimated by the Regional Production Function System*

Region	Labor	Land	Purchased inputs	Capital
Northeast 1	0.200	0.062	0.514	0.224
Northeast 2	0.335	0.142	0.240	0.284
Lake States	0.319	0.186	0.236	0.259
Corn Belt	0.307	0.168	0.256	0.269
N. Plains	-0.250	0.158	0.456	0.635
Appalachian	0.066	0.168	0.263	0.503
Southeast	0.403	0.333	0.286	-0.023
Delta States	0.342	0.191	0.323	0.144
South'n Plains	-0.240	0.148	0.401	0.699
Mountain	-0.142	0.389	0.310	0.444
Pacific	0.649	0.289	0.387	-0.324
National Avg.	*0.278*	*0.294*	*0.247*	*0.186*

At the national average (as estimated from the whole sample), output elasticities of labor and land are both slightly less than 0.30, and the elasticities for purchased inputs and capital slightly below 0.25 and 0.20. This contrasts with other estimates such as Lau and Yotopolous (1991) in their 43-country study of a meta-production function. In their study, a very high production elasticity of land (0.668) obtained assuming a Cobb-Douglas technology was reduced to 0.396 with a translog specification. But, together with the production elasticity of labor (0.403 plus 0.108 for technical education), their land elasticity remains substantially higher than our estimates. Although the elasticities obtained for livestock (0.143), machinery (0.109), and fertilizer (0.058) are lower than our estimates, Lau and Yotopolous' results point towards the existence of significant economies of scale.[9] Our national level estimates indicate a lower production elasticity of land, a higher production elasticity for purchased inputs, and the presence of constant returns to scale in conventional inputs.[10]

At a regional level, the Northeast 2, Lake State, and Corn Belt regions appear to be most representative of the national average. High elasticities of capital and purchased inputs are observed in the Northern and Southern Plains, as well as in the Appalachian and Mountain regions.[11] By contrast, high elasticities of labor, together with low production elasticity of capital in the

Southeast and the Pacific suggests that in these regions labor and purchased inputs were used to substitute for capital. The elasticity of land, which is still quite high in these two regions, is extremely low in the Northeast 1 region where purchased inputs, rather than capital, make the most important contribution to output and land's contribution is very low.[12]

The estimated rate of total factor productivity growth, obtained by evaluating equation 23 at geometric means for the sample, is 0.58% per annum. This estimate is slightly lower than the 0.79% obtained using the index number approach.[13] The second derivative of output with respect to time, b_{tt}, is significant and less than zero, suggesting that in the absence of embodiment effects, the rate of TFP growth would likely decrease over time.

At the national level, neutrality of total factor productivity growth, i.e., b_{it} = 0, ∀ i, can be rejected at the 5% level of significance, a result which is in line with virtually all studies that have tested for Hicks-neutral technical change in US agriculture (e.g., Antle 1984, Binswanger 1984, Capalbo and Denny 1986, Jorgenson et al. 1987, Capalbo and Vo 1988, and Chavas and Cox 1992). If changes in TFP are taken to be equivalent to technical change, our results imply that in the aggregate, technical change has been labor- and land-saving but capital and variable input-using. This is in agreement with the above studies concerning the variable input-using and labor-saving character of technical change in US agriculture. However, it contradicts conventional wisdom which has it that technical change has been land-using rather than land-saving. Inspection of the results for the specification that includes human capital as a separate variable indicates that productivity change has been saving in unskilled labor and capital (which, in this specification, includes land) but human capital and purchased input-using. More detailed discussion of factor biases of technical change and nonconventional factors are provided in the next chapter.

GROWTH ACCOUNTING

In order to determine the contribution of individual factors in different regions to productivity growth we can make use of the coefficients of the production function estimated at the national and regional levels to do counterfactual growth accounting as follows:[14] Let L_0, A_0, P_0, F_0, denote the quantity of inputs in the first period and L_T, A_T, P_T, F_T the quantities of inputs in the latter period, and let T be the length of the period under consideration. Then the average increase of factor productivity between periods 0 and T can be approximated as the difference between estimated production under different "technology-regimes".

Using the estimate of output that could be obtained from using initial period input quantities with period-0 and period-T technology, respectively, an estimate of the annual rate of "neutral" factor productivity growth, γ, is given by

$$\gamma_0 = \frac{1}{T}[\ln \hat{F}(L_0, A_0, P_0, F_0, T) - \ln \hat{F}(L_0, A_0, P_0, F_0, 0)] \quad (24)$$

Alternatively, one can use input quantities from the terminal period under the two technology regimes, yielding

$$\gamma_T = \frac{1}{T}[\ln \hat{F}(L_T, A_T, P_T, F_T, T) - \ln \hat{F}(L_T, A_T, P_T, F_T, 0)] \quad (25)$$

If technical change is not neutral, the two estimates will not be identical. We follow Lau and Boskin (1992) in using a simple arithmetic average to approximate the rate of factor productivity growth by $\gamma = (\gamma_0 + \gamma_T)/2$.

In a similar fashion (following, again, Lau and Boskin 1992), the contribution of any individual factor to factor productivity growth can be estimated as $\lambda = (\lambda_0 + \lambda_T)/2$, where λ_0 and λ_T are defined analogously. Using the case for labor one has

$$\lambda_0 = \frac{1}{T}[\ln \hat{F}(L_T, A_0, P_0, F_0, 0) - \ln \hat{F}(L_0, A_0, P_0, F_0, 0)] \quad (26)$$

and

$$\lambda_T = \frac{1}{T}[\ln \hat{F}(L_T, A_T, P_T, F_T, T) - \ln \hat{F}(L_0, A_T, P_T, F_T, T)] \quad (27)$$

In order to make use of all of the available data rather than rely only on estimates at the endpoints[15], we calculate the rates of "neutral" productivity growth as well as the contribution of individual inputs for each of the 11 production regions and for all consecutive years during the 1949-85 period, to obtain the average rates of the change in output due to changes in technology (T) and input use that are reported in table 3.7.

For interpretation of the estimates reported in table 3.7 it is useful to distinguish between the "gross" and the "net" contribution to output growth by any factor. The gross contribution by any factor (as presented in table 3.7), is given by the growth rate of output that can be attributed both to changes in the quantity and the productivity of this factor. We approximate the "net" contribution of individual factors by subtracting from the gross contribution increases in the factor quantity (as described in tables 2.5, 2.7, 2.8, and 2.9). It emerges that in all but the Northeast 1 and the Pacific regions, purchased inputs, followed by capital, and neutral technical progress made the most important gross contribution to output growth.

Table 3.7: *Contribution of Neutral Technical Change and Changes in Individual Factor Quantities to Output Growth as Simulated Using. Coefficients of the Production Function, by Region.*

REGION	Neutral	Labor	Land	P. Inputs	Capital
	%	%	%	%	
Northeast 1	2.679	-1.254	-3.368	-0.429	0.415
Northeast 2	1.541	-2.207	-1.119	1.810	-0.208
Lake States	-0.158	-0.919	-0.721	2.430	0.644
Corn Belt	0.058	-0.990	-1.168	2.632	0.557
Northern Plains	0.300	-0.834	0.131	2.605	0.522
Appalachian	0.086	-1.031	-2.793	1.655	0.844
Southeast	0.555	-1.913	-1.341	2.973	0.776
Delta	0.277	-1.854	-0.123	2.764	0.698
South'n Plains	-0.045	-1.130	0.223	2.123	0.741
Mountain	1.625	-2.764	-0.527	1.562	0.035
Pacific	0.749	-0.931	0.001	0.827	1.131

However, capital's net contribution to productivity growth was clearly negative. For all the regions under concern, the quantity of capital services used in agricultural production increased by more than the average annual contribution of capital services to output growth. The net contribution of purchased inputs to growth was clearly positive only in the Northeast 2, slightly positive in the Corn Belt, Lake States, and Delta regions, but clearly negative in the Mountain and Pacific regions. Labor quantity decreased at a more rapid rate than labor's contribution to output in almost all regions, suggesting that labor productivity increased considerably during the period under concern. The simulation also supports our earlier finding of low rates of "neutral" technical change and highlights the importance of embodiment of such change in inputs, in particular for the traditional agricultural regions in the mid-west.

Notes:

1. The effects of such adjustment are discussed at length in Capalbo and Vo (1988).

2. The figures compared are indexes given by Evenson, Landau, and Ballou (1987). While these are different from the growth rates reported by Huffman and Evenson (1992 and 1993) the differences do not affect the qualitative conclusions drawn here.

3. For more detailed figures refer to tables A 3.1 to A 3.3 in the appendix.

4. A dynamic non-agricultural sector might pull labor out of agriculture but would normally not lead to productivity growth as even with reduced employment, wage rates would still equal labor's marginal product.

5. Such a phenomenon, i.e., high growth of output but low growth of productivity, would result if most of output growth was due to technical progress embodied in imported capital goods for which suppliers are able to charge prices close to the goods' marginal product.

6. Differences between the two figures may result from the fact that, by treating each state as one observation, large and small states are weighted equally in the econometric assessment. In contrast, the weighting scheme used for index number construction reflects states' share in total output or input.

7. State-dummies were jointly significantly different from zero but are not reported here.

8. Such differences can be traced not only to the state-dummies but also to the differences in the mean values of the independent variables (i.e., inputs) mentioned earlier.

9. As the degree of economies of scale is increasing in the degree of mechanization, US agriculture should be characterized by especially large economies of scale.

10. Constant returns to scale could not be rejected at the 5% level of significance.

11. The four negative output elasticities in this table are likely to result from the imposition of the profit-maximization and homogeneity restrictions which, while holding for the aggregate sample, need not hold for the regional estimates.

12. Note that these results are more or less in line with the factor shares reported in appendix table A 2.2.

13. If, as demonstrated below, each year is treated as a separate observation in counterfactual growth accounting, the average annual rate of neutral factor productivity growth increases to 0.89%.

14. Originally it was intended to ascertain the contribution of factors to productivity growth in various regions by estimating a meta-production function (following Lau and Boskin 1992) with four inputs in which individual states are characterized by access to the same technology but differ in the amount of "efficiency equivalent inputs" used. However, the hypothesis of equal second order coefficients across regions was rejected at the 5% level of significance. It was therefore necessary to estimate separate functions for individual regions.

15. Calculation for the endpoints, i.e., setting period 0 equal to 1949 and period 1 equal to 1985 (with $T = 37$) proved to be quite sensitive to deviations in any of these two years.

IV

THE ECONOMIC EFFECTS OF
RESEARCH AND
EXTENSION

In this section we report our results from using a cost function framework to estimate elasticities of factor substitution and own price elasticities; to determine the bias of technical change; to provide evidence regarding the factor-biasing effect of research, extension and spillins; and to evaluate the economic benefits from local and spillin research. Results indicate that estimated elasticities are broadly in line with other studies although there are some important differences; that productivity growth was not neutral but capital-using and land-saving; that public agricultural research tended to be biased in the same direction; and that there were significant economic benefits from research, many of which were associated with research spillins rather with public agricultural research undertaken by states themselves.

METHODOLOGY

CONVENTIONAL INPUTS

The cost of production for any state i can be written as a function of the quantity of output Q_i, the factor prices w_i for labor (L_i), land (A_i), purchased inputs (P_i), and capital (P_i), and the stock of knowledge K_i, which in turn is a function of the state-specific real expenditures on research (R_i), extension, (E_i), as well as spillins (S_i). It follows that

$$C(\cdot) = C(Q_i, w_i, K_i) = C(Q_i, w_i, R_i, S_i, E_i) \quad (28)$$

We assume that factor prices, research, extension, and spillin-pools[1] are exogenous. If the same cost function holds for all 48 states, the data described above can be used to estimate this cost function using the state-specific price indexes constructed above. We control for the unobservable state-specific differences in infrastructure and intangible effects of the nonagricultural sector by including a set of 47 state-dummies. We choose a translog functional form that is specified as follows;

$$
\begin{aligned}
\ln C\,(y_i, w_i, R_i, S_i, X_i) = &\sum_{i=1}^{47} \delta_i D_i + \\
&a_L(\ln w_{Li}) + a_A(\ln w_{Ai}) + a_P(\ln w_{Pi}) + a_F(\ln w_{Fi}) + \\
&a_Y(\ln Y_i) + a_R(\ln R_i) + a_E(\ln E_i) + a_S(\ln S_i) + \\
&b_{LL}(\ln w_{Li})(\ln w_{Li}) + b_{LA}(\ln w_{Li})(\ln w_{Ai}) + b_{LP}(\ln w_{Li})(\ln w_{Pi}) + b_{LF}(\ln w_{Li})(\ln w_{Fi}) + \\
&b_{LY}(\ln w_{Li})(\ln Y_i) + b_{LR}(\ln w_{Li})(\ln R_i) + b_{LE}(\ln w_{Li})(\ln E_i) + b_{LS}(\ln w_{Li})(\ln S_i) + \\
&b_{AA}(\ln w_{Ai})(\ln w_{Ai}) + b_{AP}(\ln w_{Ai})(\ln w_{Pi}) + b_{AF}(\ln w_{Ai})(\ln w_{Fi}) + \\
&b_{AY}(\ln w_{Ai})(\ln Y_i) + b_{AR}(\ln w_{Ai})(\ln R_i) + b_{AE}(\ln w_{Ai})(\ln E_i) + b_{AS}(\ln w_{Ai})(\ln S_i) + \\
&b_{PP}(\ln w_{Pi})(\ln w_{Pi}) + b_{PF}(\ln w_{Pi})(\ln w_{Fi}) + \\
&b_{PY}(\ln w_{Pi})(\ln Y_i) + b_{PR}(\ln w_{Pi})(\ln R_i) + b_{PE}(\ln w_{Pi})(\ln E_i) + b_{PS}(\ln w_{Pi})(\ln S_i) + \\
&b_{FF}(\ln w_{Fi})(\ln w_{Fi}) + \\
&b_{FY}(\ln w_{Fi})(\ln Y_i) + b_{FR}(\ln w_{Fi})(\ln R_i) + b_{FE}(\ln w_{Fi})(\ln E_i) + b_{FS}(\ln w_{Fi})(\ln S_i) + \\
&b_{YY}(\ln Y_i)(\ln Y_i) + b_{YR}(\ln Y_i)(\ln R_i) + b_{YE}(\ln Y_i)(\ln E_i) + b_{YS}(\ln Y_i)(\ln S_i) + \\
&b_{RR}(\ln R_i)(\ln R_i) + b_{RE}(\ln E_i)(\ln E_i) + b_{RS}(\ln S_i)(\ln S_i) + \\
&b_{EE}(\ln E_i)(\ln E_i) + b_{ES}(\ln E_i)(\ln S_i) + \\
&b_{SS}(\ln S_i)(\ln S_i)
\end{aligned}
\quad (29)
$$

where $C(Q_i, w_i, R_i, S_i, E_i)$ represents aggregate cost for state i (in time period t) the D_i's are state-dummies, w_{Li}, w_{Ai}, w_{Pi}, and w_{Fi} are state specific factor prices; Q_i, R_i, S_i, and E_i are the values of aggregate output, the stock of research, the spillin pool, and annual extension expenditures for each state.

Differentiation with respect to w_{Li}, w_{Ki}, w_{Pi}, and w_{Fi} yields the four-equation system of expenditure share equations

$$s_L = a_L + b_{LL}(\ln w_{Li}) + b_{LA}(\ln w_{Ai}) + b_{LP}(\ln w_{Pi}) + b_{LF}(\ln w_{Fi}) +$$
$$b_{LY}(\ln Y_i) + b_{LR}(\ln R_i) + b_{LE}(\ln E_i) + b_{LS}(\ln S_i)$$

$$s_A = a_A + b_{AL}(\ln w_{Li}) + b_{AA}(\ln w_{Ai}) + b_{AP}(\ln w_{Pi}) + b_{AF}(\ln w_{Fi}) +$$
$$b_{AY}(\ln Y_i) + b_{AR}(\ln R_i) + b_{AE}(\ln E_i) + b_{AS}(\ln S_i)$$

$$s_P = a_P + b_{PL}(\ln w_{Li}) + b_{PA}(\ln w_{Ai}) + b_{PP}(\ln w_{Pi}) + b_{PF}(\ln w_{Fi}) + \quad (30)$$
$$b_{PY}(\ln Y_i) + b_{PR}(\ln R_i) + b_{PE}(\ln E_i) + b_{PS}(\ln S_i)$$

$$s_F = a_F + b_{FL}(\ln w_{Li}) + b_{FA}(\ln w_{Ai}) + b_{FP}(\ln w_{Pi}) + b_{FF}(\ln w_{Fi}) +$$
$$b_{FY}(\ln Y_i) + b_{FR}(\ln R_i) + b_{FE}(\ln E_i) + b_{FS}(\ln S_i)$$

If producers minimize cost, the coefficients a_i and b_{ij} in these equations are identical to the respective coefficients in the cost function. Therefore, after dropping one of the share equations to avoid singularity of the covariance-matrix, the system of four equations, i.e., the cost function plus three share equations, can be estimated using maximum likelihood methods (Barten 1967).

The marginal change in cost due to changes in factor prices or the "fixed" factors such as research and extension, can be obtained by evaluating this derivative at sample means. For the case of labor

$$\frac{\partial C}{\partial w_L} = \frac{\partial \ln C}{\partial \ln w_L} \frac{C}{\bar{w}_L} = \frac{C}{\bar{w}_L}[a_L + b_{LL}(\ln \bar{w}_L) + b_{LA}(\ln \bar{w}_A) + b_{LP}(\ln \bar{w}_P) + \quad (31)$$
$$b_{LY}(\ln \bar{Y}) + b_{LR}(\ln \bar{R}) + b_{LE}(\ln \bar{E}) + b_{LS}(\ln \bar{S})]$$

where bars denote sample means of the respective variable.

For the conventional factors of production, Allen partial elasticities of factor substitution (σ_{ij}, $i,j = L, A, P, F$) can be computed as

$$\sigma_{jk} = \frac{C C_{jk}}{C_j C_k}, \text{ i.e. } \sigma_{jk} = \frac{\beta_{jk} + s_j s_k}{s_j s_k}, j \neq k \; ; \quad \sigma_{jj} = \frac{\beta_{jj} + s_j^2 - s_j}{s_j^2}; \quad (32)$$

where $C_i = \partial C / \partial w_i$, $C_{ij} = \partial^2 C / \partial w_i \partial w_j = b_{ij}$ is the coefficient from the cost function, and s_i is factor i's share in total cost. Own and cross price elasticities of factor demand (ϵ_{ij}; $i,j = L, A, P, F$) can be obtained by multiplying the Allen elasticities by their respective factor shares, i.e., $\epsilon_{ij} = \sigma_{ij} * s_j$.

By Shephard's lemma, the demand for any conventional factor j is given by the derivative of cost with respect to the factor price so that

$$\frac{\partial C}{\partial w_i} = \frac{\partial C\,(Q_i,\,w_i,\,R_i,\,S_i,\,E_i)}{\partial w_i} \qquad (33)$$

Similarly, the short-run effect of research or extension on demand for any factor j (as well as the effect of other nonconventional inputs) is given by the second logarithmic derivative of the cost function with respect to research (or any other nonconventional inputs), $\partial^2 lnC/\partial lnw_i\partial lnR = b_{ir}$, which can be obtained directly as the coefficient from the estimated equation.

NONCONVENTIONAL INPUTS

The contribution of public research or other nonconventional inputs to growth in productivity can be approximated using two different methods:

(a) *Productivity decomposition analysis* proceeds in two distinct steps. First, an index of total factor productivity growth is computed. Then the rate of factor productivity growth thus estimated is related to certain exogenous factors in a second step using regression analysis. This method facilitates the analysis of a wide range of aspects that are directly or indirectly related to productivity growth, such as pre-technology science and private sector research investment. As a result of evaluating the effects of such measures separately from assessment of productivity growth, however, the statistical significance and economic interpretation of the estimates obtained is problematic, particularly given the problems of omitted variables and multicollinearity in any of the regression equations.

(b) *Augmented production or cost function approach*. Considering research and extension as nonconventional inputs facilitates their direct incorporation into a production function or the dual cost or profit functions. In this way, the contribution of research, together with conventional factors, to increased profits and/or reduced cost, can be calculated. Advantages of this method are that parameters for conventional and nonconventional inputs are estimated jointly, i.e., are less subject to omitted variable bias, and their comparison to results reported in the literature provides a yardstick against which to gauge the overall sensibility of the results. Furthermore, interaction effects between nonconventional and conventional inputs are provided, allowing inferences regarding the factor bias of research or other non-conventional variables.

It is important to note that econometric estimation measures the marginal benefit from research but not the distribution (e.g., between consumers and producers or between countries; see Alston, Edwards, and Freebairn 1988 or Davis, Oram, and Ryan 1989) of such benefits. The distribution depends on the structure of production as well as markets (i.e., the commodities most affected by research advances, their regional distribution, and price elasticities of demand and supply). The magnitude of benefits from research and their distribution among different groups are not totally independent from each other. For instance the lobbying efforts of various interest-groups, may well affect the character of the research program adopted and thus the benefits to be obtained from research (see, e.g., Roe and Pardey 1989, Alston and Pardey 1993). Rather than adopting a political economy framework in which these issues, including the social cost incurred through lobbying efforts, are explicitly modeled, we chose to ignore distributional issues for two reasons. First, interest groups are more likely to lobby for the provision of alternative public (or possibly more private) goods than for the allocation of resources to research in particular commodities. Inclusion of such alternative public goods would require a more comprehensive framework which can not be appropriately dealt with using the data available here. Second, if it is clear that what is analyzed here is in fact the outcome of a "lobbying-game" rather than an abstract first-best solution. So quantitative assessment of the magnitude of research benefits under this scenario may provide a starting point for discussion on the distribution of such benefits and a more comprehensive analysis of the determinants of, and assumptions required for alternative - and possibly Pareto-superior - outcomes.

In contrast to conventional factors, an increase in research investment (R_i) by any state i has, according to our specification, two types of impact. First, it directly affects cost of production in the originating state through $\partial C/\partial R_i$. Second, since a unit increase in research spending by state i increases the spillin pool available to state j by P_{ij} (with P_{ij} defined in equation 13), such an increase may also affect cost of production in other states. The appropriable ("local" or state-specific) effect of an increase in research investment is computed as

$$\rho_{local} = \frac{\partial \ln C}{\partial \ln R} \frac{C}{R} = \frac{C}{R}[a_R + b_{RL}(\ln \bar{w}_L) + b_{RA}(\ln \bar{w}_A) + b_{RP}(\ln \bar{w}_P) + b_{RF}(\ln \bar{w}_F) + \quad (34)$$
$$b_{RY}(\ln \bar{Y}) + b_{RR}(\ln \bar{R}) + b_{RE}(\ln \bar{E}) + b_{RS}(\ln \bar{S})]$$

The magnitude of spillover-effects, measured here as the returns to research undertaken by state i which come about via spillovers to other states j, depends

not only on the symmetric matrix of spillover coefficients, P_{ij}, but also on the
level of the independent variables such as research and extension in each of the
receiving states. These spillover effects are given by

$$\rho_{spillover} = \sum_{j \neq i}^{48} P_{ij} \frac{\partial \ln C_i}{\partial \ln S_j} \frac{C_i}{S_j} =$$

$$\sum_{j \neq i}^{48} P_{ij} \left[(a_S + b_{SL}(\ln \bar{w}_{Lj}) + b_{SA}(\ln \bar{w}_{Aj}) + b_{SP}(\ln \bar{w}_{Pj}) + b_{SF}(\ln \bar{w}_{Fj}) + \right. \tag{35}$$

$$\left. b_{SY}(\ln \bar{Y}_j) + b_{SR}(\ln \bar{R}_j) + b_{SE}(\ln \bar{E}_j) + b_{SS}(\ln \bar{S}_j) \right] \frac{C_i}{S_j}$$

The overall cost reducing effect of research, i.e., the local and spillout or non-
local effects of research carried out in a particular state is given by the sum of
ρ_{local} and $\rho_{spillover}$. Given ρ_{local} and $\rho_{spillover}$, together with specific assumptions
concerning the lag length (L_R) and the temporal weights w_t which indicate the
distribution of knowledge-effects over time, the local and social internal rates of
return to research can be calculated as the values of r_p and r_s which solve,
respectively[2]

$$\sum_{t=0}^{L_R} \frac{w_t \, \rho_{local}}{(1+r_p)^t} = 1.0 ; \quad \sum_{t=0}^{L_R} \frac{w_t \, (\rho_{local} + \rho_{spillover})}{(1+r_s)^t} = 1.0 ; \tag{36}$$

RESULTS

Estimated coefficients for the cost function including nonconventional inputs but
excluding dummies are summarized in table 4.1. The specification is characterized by high explanatory power and statistical significance.[3] Evaluation of the
formula for marginal cost elasticities at means for the whole sample, for
production regions, individual states, or specific years facilitates exploration of
the marginal cost effects of changes in prices, output, and nonconventional
inputs at different levels of disaggregation. With the exception of purchased
inputs, the cost elasticity of which is not significantly different from zero, almost
all of these cost elasticities with respect to input price changes have the
expected, positive, sign. Use of sample means for different years indicates that,
during the 1949-85 period, cost elasticities with respect to labor decreased from
0.28 to -0.04 whereas the cost elasticity for land decreased from over 0.26 to
0.14 between 1949 and 1985. By contrast, the cost elasticity of purchased inputs
was characterized by a large increase over time.

Table 4.1: *Coefficients of the Cost Function as Estimated from the System of Equations*

Variable	Estimate	Std.Err.	t-value
Intercept	12.814	3.237	3.958
P_{Labor}	-0.659	0.340	-1.938
P_{Land}	1.761	0.212	8.289
$P_{P.Inputs}$	0.292	0.352	0.829
$P_{Capital}$	-0.394	0.047	-8.455
Output	0.212	0.339	0.625
Research	0.114	0.547	0.209
Extension	2.626	0.605	4.337
Spillover	-1.982	0.666	-2.976
P_{Labor} x P_{Labor}	0.122	0.013	9.238
P_{Labor} x P_{Land}	-0.053	0.012	-4.410
P_{Labor} x $P_{P.Inputs}$	-0.035	0.007	-4.949
P_{Labor} x $P_{Capital}$	-0.034	0.005	-7.152
P_{Labor} x Output	0.252	0.031	8.056
P_{Labor} x Research	-0.282	0.047	-5.990
P_{Labor} x Extension	0.205	0.054	3.816
P_{Labor} x Spillover	-0.190	0.043	-4.375
P_{Land} x P_{Land}	0.038	0.011	3.465
P_{Land} x $P_{P.Inputs}$	0.008	0.006	1.310
P_{Land} x $P_{Capital}$	0.007	0.003	2.650
P_{Land} x Output	-0.036	0.017	-2.143
P_{Land} x Research	0.011	0.022	0.490
P_{Land} x Extension	0.069	0.021	3.370
P_{Land} x Spillover	-0.155	0.018	-8.721
$P_{P.Inputs}$ x $P_{P.Inputs}$	-0.011	0.010	-1.085
$P_{P.Inputs}$ x $P_{Capital}$	0.037	0.005	7.515
$P_{P.Inputs}$ x Output	-0.126	0.018	-6.945
$P_{P.Inputs}$ x Research	-0.016	0.034	-0.474
$P_{P.Inputs}$ x Extension	0.074	0.036	2.041
$P_{P.Inputs}$ x Spillover	0.078	0.033	2.370
$P_{Capital}$ x $P_{Capital}$	-0.010	0.007	-1.485
$P_{Capital}$ x Output	-0.090	0.031	-2.886
$P_{Capital}$ x Research	0.217	0.049	4.428
$P_{Capital}$ x Extension	-0.241	0.056	-4.326
$P_{Capital}$ x Spillover	0.178	0.025	6.987
Output x Output	-0.018	0.007	-2.780
Output x Research	-0.110	0.022	-4.976
Output x Extension	0.156	0.018	8.616
Output x Spillover	0.013	0.030	0.437
Research x Research	0.220	0.020	10.720
Research x Extension	-0.226	0.029	-7.765
Research x Spillover	-0.024	0.046	-0.519
Extension x Extension	0.048	0.017	2.763
Extension x Spillover	-0.294	0.050	-5.878
Spillover x Spillover	0.175	0.040	4.346

ELASTICITIES OF FACTOR SUBSTITUTION AND DEMAND

Allen elasticities of factor substitution and own- and cross- price elasticities of demand, together with their standard errors, are presented in table 4.2.

Table 4.2: *Allen Elasticities of Factor Substitution*

	Labor	Land	Purchased Inputs	Capital
Labor	-1.05316	-0.1109	0.64395	0.11301
	(0.1159)	(0.0817)	(0.0068)	(0.0930)
Land	-0.1109	-3.1206	1.10739	1.21996
	(0.0817)	(0.2032)	(0.0341)	(0.0401)
Purchased Inputs	0.64395	1.10739	-1.5538	2.10699
	(0.0068)	(0.0341)	(0.0469)	(0.0205)
Capital	0.11301	1.21996	2.10699	-5.6829
	(0.0930)	(0.0401)	(0.0205)	(0.0751)

Note:　　Numbers in parentheses are standard errors.

　　　　The signs on the own price elasticities are all negative as expected. Positive signs on the cross-price elasticities indicate pairwise substitution between inputs with the exception of labor and land, which are complements. The corresponding own- and cross-price elasticities of factor demand are presented in table 4.3.

Table 4.3: *Own and Cross Price Elasticities of Demand*

	Labor	Land	Purchased Inputs	Capital
Labor	-0.25526	-0.02178	0.25907	0.01797
	(0.0281)	(0.0160)	(0.0027)	(0.0148)
Land	-0.02689	-0.6126	0.44552	0.19398
	(0.0160)	(0.0399)	(0.0137)	(0.0033)
Purchased Inputs	0.15608	0.21739	-0.62511	0.33502
	(0.0016)	(0.0067)	(0.0189)	(0.0033)
Capital	0.02739	0.23949	0.84767	-0.9036
	(0.0148)	(0.0079)	(0.0082)	(0.0119)

Note: Numbers in parentheses are standard errors.

Compared to other studies, these estimates point towards relatively high substitutability not only between purchased inputs and land but also between such inputs and labor and capital. Thus, purchased inputs may substitute for land[4] but also for labor.

Table 4.4 compares the own price elasticities estimated here to the estimates obtained by other studies.

Table 4.4: *Comparison of our Results to Own Price Elasticities of Demand Obtained by Other Studies*

Study	Labor	Land	Capital	Pur. Input
Antle (1984)	-0.01	-0.18	-0.25	-0.25
Binswanger (1974)	-0.91	-0.34	-1.09	-0.95
Brown/Christensen (1981)	-0.66		-0.05	-0.20
Hazilla/Koop (1986)	-0.96		-0.52	-0.54
Huffman/Evenson (1989)	-0.51		-0.61	-0.71[a] -1.20[b]
Lopez (1980)	-0.52	-0.42	-0.35	-0.41
Ray (1982)	-0.85		-0.53	-0.40
Shumway (1983)	-0.43		-0.37	-0.70
Our Result	-0.26	-0.61	-0.90	-0.63

[a] Refers to fuel and pesticides.
[b] Refers to fertilizer.

The most striking difference to other studies concerns the elasticities for labor and land. With the exception of Antle (1984), who obtains very inelastic demand for labor, the estimated own price elasticities of labor demand range from -0.43 (Shumway, 1983 for the whole US) to -1.085 (Villezca-Becerra and Shumway 1992 for TX). Considering, however, that most of the studies such as Brown and Christensen (1981), Hazilla and Koop (1986), Lopez (1980), Ray (1982), and Villezca-Becerra and Shumway (1992) estimated the elasticity of demand for hired labor while our figure includes hired, operator, and family labor, the estimate obtained here, which is considerably lower, is plausible.

The few studies which estimated price elasticity of demand for land, obtained elasticities between -0.18 and -0.42, lower than the -0.61 estimated here. As our data covers a longer time period in contrast to the other studies whose data does often not extend into the 1980s, and includes periods in which government programs were of higher importance, such an estimate appears reasonable. A price elasticity of demand for capital that is more elastic than the price elasticity of demand for purchased inputs is in line with results reported by Binswanger (1974), Ray (1982), and the recent, regional-level study by Villezca-Becerra and Shumway (1992). Differentiating between capital and machinery, the latter study reports own price elasticities of demand ranging from -0.68 (for capital in FL) to -1.67 (for machinery in TX) and obtained elastic demand for machinery (though not for capital) in all four of the states studied. By contrast, their own price elasticities of demand for fertilizer, pesticides, and "miscellaneous" range from -0.57 (for fertilizer in IA) to -0.032 (for fertilizer in CA). We obtain elasticities for capital and purchased inputs that, while still inelastic, are comparatively high and only slightly lower than the estimates obtained by Binswanger(1974).[5]

FACTOR BIAS

Use of the dual cost rather than the primal production function to assess biases of productivity growth is preferable on economic and statistical grounds because factor prices are more likely to be exogenously determined than input quantities, thus reducing the potential for simultaneous equation bias and/or multicollinearity across explanatory variables. We first use a simple time trend specification, analogous to the production function discussed above, to determine the factor bias nature of technical change. As Binswanger (1974) showed, for a time-trend specification such as this, the biased nature of technical change with respect to any factor i is given by $\partial s_i / \partial t$, i.e., the derivative of the share equation with respect to time. Numerical values obtained for $\partial s_i / \partial t$, as obtained from the joint estimation of the cost function and associated share equations for each of the production regions, are summarized in table 4.5. A negative coefficient implies that productivity growth was saving in the input while a positive number implies the presence of factor using bias.

The most important deviation of these figures from results obtained by other studies is that, in the aggregate, technical change was land-saving rather than land-using, a result that has been obtained by studies of technical change in US agriculture (Antle 1984; Hayami and Ruttan 1985).[6] Neutrality of technical change with respect to land can not be rejected in the Corn Belt, Lake, Northern Plain, Mountain and Pacific states, and a land-saving bias prevails in the South (Appalachian, Delta, and Southeast regions) and the Northeast. A land-using bias can be confirmed only for the Southern Plains region. Cox and

Chavas (1990) represent the only study in the literature which also finds evidence for land-saving technical change in US agriculture. Their findings are based on a non-parametric approach and they interpret their results as indicating that the export-driven agriculture during the mid- and late-1970s was character-ized by land-saving technical change. Archibald and Brandt (1991) found that Japanese agriculture was also characterized by weakly land-saving technical change.

Table 4.5: *Factor Biases of Technical Change in Individual Production Regions as Determined by Cost Function Estimation*

Region	Land	Labor	Capital	Purchased In-puts
Northeast 1	-0.0089	-0.0269	ns[a]	0.0369
Northeast 2	-0.0077	-0.0138	0.0104	ns
Lake States	ns	-0.0123	0.0058	0.0107
Corn Belt	ns	-0.0151	0.0148	0.0079
Northern Plains	ns	ns	0.0157	ns
Appalachian	-0.0401	-0.0201	0.0105	0.0497
Southeast	-0.0076	ns	0.0082	ns
Delta States	-0.0139	ns	0.0106	0.0117
South'n Plains	0.0090	-0.0232	ns	ns
Mountain	ns	ns	-0.0103	0.0382
Pacific	ns	-0.0134	ns	ns

[a] "ns" means that the coefficient is not significant at least at the 5% level of confidence.

In line with most other studies which find US agricultural development to be labor-saving, such bias is found to exist in seven of the eleven production regions. No significant labor-saving bias was evident for the Southeast and Delta, or for the Mountain and Northern Plains regions. In these regions, changes in relative factor prices would be sufficient to explain the observed reductions in labor input once quality-changes in the composition of the labor force have been taken into account.

With respect to capital, neutrality prevails in three states, while technical change is capital-saving in the Mountain states and capital-using in the

North-Central and Southeastern states. Neutrality of productivity change with respect to purchased capital cannot be rejected for about half of the sample, while it is found to be capital using in the rest. The Lake, Corn Belt, Appalachian, and Delta states are characterized by technical change which is using in both purchased inputs and fixed capital.

INDUCED INNOVATION

The tendency of public agricultural research systems to develop technology in order to save relatively expensive (i.e., relatively scarce) factors, and the ensuing importance of levels or changes of factor prices for the factor-biasing character of technical change, is central to the induced innovation hypothesis (Hayami and Ruttan 1985).

Recently it has been claimed that the strong empirical support for this hypothesis in US agriculture is due to Hayami and Ruttan's use of aggregated national data (Olmstead and Rhode 1993). It is argued that national averages were heavily influenced by the settlement of the land-abundant interior states and consequently reflected the rapidly increasing land-labor ratios in these states, do not convey an accurate picture of the development of US agriculture as a whole. In contrast to the aggregate national evidence, Olmstead and Rhode's view is that the majority of US regions was characterized by stable or even declining land-labor ratios and the use of disaggregated data provides only limited support for, and even a rejection of, the induced innovation hypothesis. Thus, it is maintained, that Hayami and Ruttan's failure to use regional or state-level data, together with a number of historical inaccuracies in the qualitative evidence they presented to support that empirical work led them to overstate the effect that price-induced, demand-side considerations had on the pattern of US agricultural development, while neglecting the relevance of technology supply factors, and in particular the importance of biological innovations that were forthcoming during the earliest days of US agriculture.

While we do not have evidence for the period before 1949, our data provide a more complete basis than that used by Olmstead and Rhode to assess the importance of price-induced factor substitution in the post-World War II period. Paralleling the procedure used by Hayami and Ruttan, we regressed the ratios of capital (machinery) and labor, Q_{FC}/Q_{LB}, purchased inputs and land Q_{PC}/Q_{LD}, and -in addition to Hayami and Ruttan- purchased inputs and labor Q_{PC}/Q_{LD} on the labor-land price ratio, P_{LB}/P_{LD}, and the respective factor price ratio namely P_{FC}/P_{LB}, P_{PC}/P_{LD}, and P_{PC}/P_{LD}. Frisvold (1992) showed that under the assumption of a CES production function, the estimated coefficients are equal to the substitution elasticity between the two factors under concern.

A critical issue in performing these tests of the induced innovation hypothesis relates to the inclusion of state-specific, fixed effects in the estimated relationships. Presence of such effects (i.e., state dummies) would imply that factor-price ratios are being used to explain only the temporal variation in factor quantity ratios whereas in their absence factor-price ratios would account for cross-sectional variation as well. We first estimated the model with neither state-specific effects nor time-dummies. Compared with the regressions in which both these dummy-variables are included (see below), these specifications are characterized by lower explanatory power. But, for the regressions involving the capital-labor and the purchased input-labor ratio (equations one and three, respectively, in table 4.6) coefficients on the purchased input- and land-labor price ratios have the expected signs and are highly significant. This suggests that, for the sample of US states, a large part of the cross-sectional variation in capital-labor and input-labor ratios is explained by the relative factor-price ratios but that there has been no clear relative price effect with regard to the input-land ratio. Below we show that a similar result is obtained if state and time-specific dummy-variables are included.

To address the question of the induced-innovation theory's purported failure to explain intertemporal variation in relative factor use (see Olmstead and Rhode 1993), we reestimated the model with time- and state-dummies. Significant time dummies would indicate an underlying secular trend in factor substitution that could be interpreted as resulting more directly from technical rather than price determinants, i.e., reflecting the supply- rather than the demand-side of technology. State-dummies, in turn, would capture state-specific effects such as the relative position of a state on a national meta-isoquant relative to other states which, as indicated above, is likely to have emerged in response to specific initial factor endowments and/or price ratios. Regression with both sets of dummy-variables measures whether, given the initial position of a state on the isoquant, and "autonomous" (but not necessarily Hicks-neutral) shifts of the isoquant due to technical progress, intertemporal changes in factor price ratios prompted factor substitution along the lines suggested by the induced innovation hypothesis. A summary of results from the regressions with state-dummies is presented in Table 4.6

Table 4.6:   *Summary of Regressions of Capital-labor, Input-land, and Input-labor Ratio on Factor price ratios, with State Dummies; Including Test Statistics.*

	Capital/Labor ratio		P. Input/Land ratio		P. Input/Labor ratio	
	Est. Coeff.	t value	Est. Coeff.	t value	Est. Coeff.	t value
Equation Number	1		2		3	
Intercept	-1.4813	-19.23	-0.2192	-2.61	-0.0909	-0.72
Factor price ratio[a]	-0.3122	-4.76	-0.1219	-1.24	-0.9963	-6.74
Land-Labor price ratio	-0.1507	-7.43	-0.0992	-1.06	-0.0423	-1.73
F-Value	401.16		1686.45		372.01	
R^2 (adj)	0.95		0.99		0.95	
Durbin-Watson	2.26		1.91		1.90	
Test state-dummies[b]	103.08		1555.72		237.85	
Test year-dummies	30.38		34.79		45.04	

[a] The factor-price ratio is a ratio of the prices of the factors that appear as dependent variables in the regression.
[b] Value of the F-test for the null hypothesis that all dummy-variables are equal to zero. The high value of these statistics leads to the rejection of the null hypothesis in all cases.

All three equations are statistically satisfactory and the state- and year-dummies (the latter are all positive but not reported here) are jointly significantly different from zero. This implies that state-specific, fixed effects are significant for all three factor ratios. Furthermore, given the sign of the time dummies, there appears to be an autonomous increase in the capital-labor, the input-land, and the input-labor ratios that was independent of changes in relative factor prices. The sign and significance of state dummies suggest that technical change was not Hicks-neutral but capital and purchased input using. This allows us to turn to the effects of changes in factor-price ratios[7] on the observed input-quantity ratios.

The *land-labor price ratio* which according to the induced-innovation hypothesis has a significant impact on the factor bias of technical change in the long run, is significant at the 5% level only in equation number one but not in the other two. Thus, after correcting for state- and time-specific effects, a relative increase in land prices would be associated with a lower use of capital. Similarly, increases in labor prices would lead to more capital intensive forms of production. By contrast, neither the input/land nor the input/labor ratio appear to have responded significantly to changes in land and/or labor prices.

Factor price ratios are significant in equations 1 and 3, but not in equation 2. This indicates that, while changes in input and/or land prices did not lead to changes in the input/land ratio (equation 2), decreases in the relative prices of capital and purchased inputs were associated with the expected substitution of the relatively cheaper for the dearer input (equations 1 and 3). The high degree of substitutability between purchased inputs and labor is particularly surprising. If such a relationship also holds for other countries, changes in relative prices might have far-reaching implications for relative factor intensities not only in the long term but also in the short term.

To summarize;

(a) Long-term, cross-sectional variation in input intensities is in line with the predictions of the induced innovation hypothesis concerning the ratios of capital and purchased inputs with respect to labor, but not with respect to the input/land ratio.

(b) In the short term, relative price movements are a significant determinant of the labor intensity of production but not of the intensity of land use. While the induced-innovation hypothesis has focused on substitution of capital for labor, the substitution of purchased inputs for labor appears to have been more important for the sample considered here. Based on the estimated coefficients, policies affecting the capital-labor and/or input-labor price ratios would be expected to induce empirically significant substitution effects among these inputs.
(c) Substitution of purchased inputs for land appears to be less affected by relative price movements and to be driven more by "autonomous" supply-side factors.

RETURNS TO LOCAL AND SPILLIN RESEARCH

Recall that using Shephard's lemma, the impact of local and spillin research (extension) on the demand for any factor is given by $\partial^2 C / \partial w \partial R$ (or $\partial^2 C / \partial w \partial E$, $\partial^2 C / \partial w \partial S$), i.e., the respective coefficient b_{ir}, b_{ie} or b_{is}) in the cost function. Inspection of the coefficients for nonconventional inputs in the cost function, which are summarized in table 4.7, indicates that public agricultural research (both directly and via spillin-effects) has been strongly labor-saving and capital-using. By contrast, extension tended to be capital-saving but labor- and land-using.

Table 4.7: *Marginal Effects of Nonconventional Inputs on Factor Demand*

	Effect on demand for			
	Labor	Land	Purchased Inputs	Capital
Local Research	-0.2818	0.0106	-0.0160	0.2170
	(-5.99)	(0.49)	(-0.47)	(4.43)
Spillin research	-0.1903	-0.1549	0.0778	0.1779
	(-4.38)	(-8.72)	(2.37)	(6.99)
Extension	0.2054	0.0691	0.0739	-0.2407
	3.82)	(3.37)	(2.04)	(-4.33)

Note: Figures in parentheses are t-values.

Neutrality of local research (i.e., research performed within the state) with respect to land and purchased inputs can not be rejected given that the respective coefficient is not significantly different from zero. Spillover effects are significantly land-saving and variable input-using. This result is in line with those reported by Binswanger et al. (1987) who use cross-country data to find that research (in total) has been land-saving. Note, however, that higher significance of spillovers may also reflect the possibility that the spillin variable picks up part of the effects of private research.

Calculation of the marginal cost effects for nonconventional inputs shows that these effects are negative and significantly different from zero throughout. Thus, as would be expected, local and spillin research, along with extension all reduce the cost of production.

Using the coefficients from the estimated cost function, calculating the marginal products of nonconventional inputs using equation 34 is straightforward. Given the marginal product, we calculate the (appropriable) *local rate of return to research* by evaluating the cash flow resulting from the investment of one dollar in research at time t over the ensuing L_R years, where L_R represents the lag length. Under the assumptions made above, such an investment increases the stock of local knowledge at time $t+i$ by w_i percent, where w_i is the weight of research expenditures i years ago (which is illustrated graphically in figure 2.1). Simple multiplication of the (constant) marginal product of research with w_i yields the monetary return in year $t+i$ to a research investment of one dollar in year t. Evaluation of the resulting cash flow over all years facilitates calculation of the local rate of return to research investment.

The same method can be used to compute values for the *social rate of return* to research investment, i.e., local benefits plus the benefits to other states from research performed locally. As indicated in equation 35, a unit investment in research by state i increases the spillin-pool for state j by P_{ij}. We use a representative state (in conjunction with the set of weights w_i, $i = 1..L_R$) to compute the spillout-effect and evaluate equations 34 and 35 at the sample means to compute the cost reducing effect via spillover-effects in any period and then evaluate the cash-flow in order to obtain an estimate of the rate of return.

It was noted above that the internal rate of return to research investment is sensitive to the particular lag structure chosen. Since there is no convincing empirical or even conceptual justification for any of the lag structures discussed in the literature, we chose the lag structures used by Huffman and Evenson (1989) and the structure for public research ascertained by Cox and Chavas (1992) as two illustrative cases (see figure 2.1 for details).

It was noted above that omission of a private research variable is likely to bias upward the spillin variable which, at the aggregate level, is almost perfectly collinear to private research expenditures. This would imply that only part of the measured effects of spillins may actually be attributable to public research investment. To account for this bias, we also calculate the "social" IRR to research investment under the assumption that only half of the "spillin benefits" is due to public sector agricultural research. Results from both calculations are presented in table 4.8.

Table 4.8:   *Local and Social Internal Rates of Return to Research Investment with Different Lags and Biases, as Determined from Cost Function Estimates*

Lag		Omitted variable bias	Whole sample	Pre-1970 period	Post-1970 period
H&E	Local return	0	251.44	269.70	92.53
H&E	Social return	0	386.41	353.66	208.41
H&E	Difference		53.68	31.13	125.23
H&E	Social return	50	325.99	314.49	161.31
H&E	Difference		29.65	16.61	74.32
C&C	Local return	0	43.64	45.00	27.22
C&C	Social return	0	52.52	50.57	40.16
C&C	Difference		20.34	12.39	47.55
C&C	Social return	50	48.84	48.09	35.73
C&C	Difference		11.91	6.88	31.29

These figures lead to a number of conclusions:

(a) The choice of lag structure has a considerable impact on the calculated rate of return to research. For the whole sample (assuming no bias), the social return to research is 52% with the Cox and Chavas lag, compared with 386% with the Huffman and Evenson lag. While this large difference provides a strong justification for further research on the temporal distribution of research effects, the high estimated rate of return using the H&E lag (which is more representative of the lag specifications traditionally used in these types of analyses) also suggests that the own research variable may be biased upward due to the omission of variables measuring the availability of complementary public goods such as roads, health services, and education.

(b) The social returns to research were significantly higher than local returns for the total sample, as well as for individual periods. Under the most conservative scenario, i.e., assuming a zero bias of the coefficient on the research variable and a 50% upward bias of the coefficient on the spillin variable, social returns were still 20% (for the H&E lag) or 11% (for the C&C lag) higher than the corresponding local returns in the aggregate sample. This difference increases to 54% and 20%, respectively, if spillin and research are assumed to be affected by the same degree of bias.

(c) Both social and local returns to research declined over time, i.e., increases in the research intensity ratio were offset by a reduction of the coefficients on research and spillin-effects obtained from econometric estimation. However, social returns decreased much less than local ones. As a result the estimated difference between social and local returns for the post-1970 period was three to four times higher than the same difference in the pre-1970 period. Such a widening of the gap between appropriable and nonappropriable returns to research could provide a strong argument for research funding arrangements that devote more attention to spillin effects.

Notes:

1. Studies such as Guttman (1978), Huffman and Miranowski (1981), and Rose-Ackerman and Evenson (1985) come to conflicting conclusions regarding the endogeneity of agricultural extension expenditure and do not provide a compelling case for the need to consider extension and/or research expenditures as endogenous. Since research expenditure is not a decision variable for the individual firm, we can, in contrast to recent analyses of the topic in the literature on industrial research which treat the stocks of research and capital as quasi-fixed factors in a dynamic model (Mohnen, Nadiri and Prucha 1986, Bernstein and Nadiri 1989), take research expenditures to be exogenous as well.

2. This specification implicitly assumes that own research and spillins affect production in any state with the same lag structure. Given the limited evidence on this subject, the relatively high mobility of knowledge, especially in the public sector, and the lengthy used here wherein the full impact of research is attained only after 9 years, this appears to be a tolerable assumption. Moreover, any alternative assumptions would necessarily be based on very thin empirical evidence.

3. For the cost function (single equation), we have $R^2 = 0.997$, and $F = 7417$; the system weighted R^2 equals 0.9887.

4. Note that price-induced substitution between purchased inputs and land was held to be the main mechanism of productivity growth under conditions of land scarcity (and

with continuing low labor productivity) in Japanese agriculture by the induced innovation hypothesis.

5. Note that these elasticities were based on estimation of share-equations only.

6. Hayami and Ruttan admit that their finding of land-using technical change in the presence of increasing land prices during the post-World War II period is something of an anomaly and may be a reflection of inadequacies in the data.

7. Visual inspection of the data indicates that there is temporal variation in these factor price ratios, even within individual states, over time.

V

CONCLUSION

In this section we summarize the main results of the foregoing analysis, draw attention to questions for further research, and highlight policy conclusions that might emerge from this study.

RESULTS

(a) Lower but more uniform rates of productivity growth

Quality adjusted data lead to an estimated growth rate of TFP in US agriculture of about 0.8% annually. This growth rate is significantly lower than that reported in other studies. Adjustments for the increased quality of human and physical capital over time are a key factor leading to lower residual productivity growth. The rate of productivity growth is also more uniform across states, suggesting that the ability of states to access a common pool of technology might be an important determinant of productivity growth.

(b) Embodied technical change

Embodiment of technical change in improved inputs, in particular human capital, machinery, and purchased inputs, is found to be an important determinant of output growth. This finding is in line with results from recent economy-wide studies of productivity growth. Comparing across states, capital-deepening alone was not associated with higher productivity growth, suggesting that a large part of the returns to improved capital inputs was appropriated by other sectors of the economy. Growth accounting exercises indicate that the most important net contribution to productivity growth was made by increases in the quality-adjusted labor input.

(c) Factor bias of research

Technical change in agriculture was characterized by significant factor biases at the national and the regional level. In the aggregate, productivity growth in general (i.e., modeled as a time-trend) and agricultural research in particular have been labor- and land-saving but capital-and purchased input-using. Given increasing prices for land and labor relative to capital and purchased inputs over the period, the substitution of purchased inputs and capital for labor and land, respectively, is in line with the induced-innovation hypothesis.

(d) Productivity convergence

There is evidence of convergence in total factor productivity across states. The initial level of labor productivity which figures prominently in comparative, cross-country analyses of productivity patterns, (which often use per capita income as a proxy for labor productivity) is, however, neither the only nor the most powerful variable explaining convergence. Changes in the local stock of knowledge, the spillin-pool, and input quantities were major factors explaining differential growth of total factor productivity across states. The importance of a common stock of knowledge is highlighted by the fact that quantitatively, changes in the spillin-pool were almost ten times as important for observed rates of productivity growth as changes in the knowledge stock due to local research.

(e) Public-good characteristics of research

The pool of commonly accessible knowledge not only makes a significant contribution to growth but also gives rise to major reductions in cost of production. Our results suggest that over time, as agriculture has become more human capital intensive, the relative importance of spillovers has increased. This suggests there are significant complementarities between investments in the human capital that enhances farmers' capacity to search and screen for new technologies and investments in research aimed to increase the stock of knowledge in agriculture. As a result, social rates of return to agricultural research investment were consistently higher than the locally appropriable returns to research. The magnitude of this difference depends on particular assumptions concerning the lag structure of research effects and the potential bias due to omitted variables, all of which merit further investigation. The implied public-good characteristics of research can provide an economically rational explanation for the phenomenon of "underfunding" and may have implications for mechanisms used to secure optimal levels of research funding.

QUESTIONS FOR FURTHER RESEARCH

(a) Spillover measurement

Representation of the own knowledge stock in any state as a linear combination of lagged, local research expenditures and of the spillover-pool as the weighted sum of own knowledge stocks across all other states is based on assumptions that seem more plausible than those commonly used to date, but which have not been subjected to elaborate tests. As the purpose of the spillin matrix is to measure closeness in "technology space", data on research outputs by state, rather than output of commodities, may provide a more meaningful basis to construct this matrix at the aggregate level. This, as well as the issues of modeling technical change (see, e.g., Martin and Alston 1992), and the incorporation of spillover effects at the operational level, are areas which deserve increased attention.

(b) Optimal levels of research investment: Determination and implementation

The study shows that a mix of state- and federal funding in the US agricultural research system has generated continuously high returns to research well in excess of the cost of capital. Given the impact of the lag structure on the estimated returns to agricultural research, a better understanding of the distribution of research impacts over time is important if "socially optimal" levels of research investment are to be determined. If, as suggested here, deviations from the optimal level of such investment are due to limited appropriability of research results, the effects of particular funding mechanisms on the aggregate amount of agricultural research undertaken (as analyzed by Huffman and Evenson 1993) would merit more attention. In this case, funding mechanisms that stimulate additional contributions to agricultural research from both state and federal sources may lead to higher productivity growth. In this context, methods to determine the extent of spillover-effects more precisely and to incorporate them into ex-ante research planning (as suggested by Pardey and Wood 1992) may have some merit.

(c) Private research

More detailed examination of the contribution of private research to productivity growth, and an assessment of the respective advantages and possible complementarities between publicly and privately executed research is warranted given (i) the large amount of resources spent for private agricultural research, (ii) the observed correlation between private research investment and the spillin variable, and (iii) the fact that in US agriculture part of technical change was associated with the more intensive use of purchased inputs and capital which have largely been supplied by the private sector. The conservative approach chosen above, i.e., to account for potential upward bias of the spillover-coefficient through its correlation with private research provides conservative estimates of the returns to research investment. An alternative explanation is that public research, by providing the knowledge basis for the private sector, facilitates private research investment. More detailed evidence on this issue would be desirable. This would include determining whether the correlation between private research and the spillin variable in the aggregate persists if both variables are disaggregated by commodity and/or area of research; and to provide an indication for the direction of causality between public and private spending on research.

(d) Embodiment

The importance of embodiment, modeled here as technical progress associated with changes in the quality of inputs, implies that issues of education and hence the vintage distribution of human and physical capital are important determinants of the rate of productivity growth that can be achieved at any point in time. While this result on its own has potentially important policy-implications, a more detailed understanding of the interaction between the effects of research and the other determinants of investment patterns and productivity growth could be gained by endogenizing investment and education decisions (as modeled, for instance, by Findlay and Kierzkowski 1983, or Grossman and Helpman 1991) and to estimate the ensuing system of reduced form equations in a cost- or profit-function framework using instrumental variable techniques.

(e) Research and other public goods

If much of what was attributed to residual productivity by other studies is in fact the result of quality improvements embodied in inputs such as capital and labor, public goods such as education, health services, and infrastructure which are complementary to agricultural research, may assume increased importance as determinants of technical change in agriculture. Interactions between these variables and research which could provide a basis for policy recommendations regarding the relative importance of such public goods in comparison to research are still imperfectly understood. In a cross-country study of productivity growth, Binswanger et al. (1987) obtain highly significant coefficients on "structural shifters", but insignificance (or even negative signs) for the research and extension variables. The data set used here, together with data on the educational, physical, and financial infrastructure in the US, which are easily accessible, can be used to determine the effects of such public goods and their interaction with research. This would make it possible to test for the significance and extent to which the measured effects of local and spillin research reported in our analysis are biased due to the omission of such variables.

IMPLICATIONS

(a) Human capital

This study has clearly demonstrated that quality adjustment leads to estimates of productivity growth which differ significantly form those reported by other studies. High importance of human capital is indicated by the significant reduction in the estimated rate of residual productivity growth once proper adjustments for labor quality are made, and by growth accounting exercises which indicate that labor has made the most important net contribution to productivity growth in post-war US agriculture. The important contribution that improvements in the quality of the rural labor-force makes to productivity growth suggests that, even in developed countries like the US, improving the educational attainment of the rural labor force continues to generate high payoffs. Our findings reinforce the notion that a high priority be placed on rural education in developing countries, a point that was made most eloquently by Schultz (1964) and repeated by many others since. The increasing relative importance of research spillovers, which comes together with higher educational attainment of the agricultural labor force, suggests that there is some degree of substitutability between the provision of location-specific technology and rural education, an issue which has important implications for the design of appropriate agricultural research policy in developing countries.

(b) Technical change and government policies

The significant productivity effects of embodied technical change found in this study imply that the *imitation* of available knowledge by individual economic agents (as modeled, for instance, in Schmitz 1991) may be at least equal in importance to the *generation* of new knowledge which has been emphasized in most models of endogenous growth (e.g., Romer 1986 and 1989). This draws attention to the opportunities provided by the educational, physical, and financial infrastructure for individual agents to invest in implementing or engage in innovative and productive activities, rather than rent-seeking behavior, as important determinants of productivity growth (Baumol 1988 and Murphy Schleifer and Vishny 1993). Government policies affecting any of these factors are likely to have important long-term implications.

If the relatively high elasticity of substitution across factors in response to changes in relative factor prices obtained here are at all relevant for developing countries, then government-induced changes in factor price ratios (e.g., via distorted exchange rates), will have important implications concerning the evolution of agricultural technology in such countries.

(c) Spillovers and the organization of public agricultural research

Persistent differences in the input- and output-mix across regions and states indicate that a basic infrastructure that supports local research activities and which makes it possible to meet local contingencies and adapt existing technology to the particular needs and factor endowments of a region, can make a significant contribution to sustainable growth of productivity. On the other hand, the ability of individual research systems to draw on a common pool of knowledge has apparently been one of the main factors underlying the rapid productivity growth in US agriculture since 1949 and has increased in relative importance over time. If, as suggested by this study, research spillovers make an important contribution to productivity growth and reduce the cost of production, funding decisions for public agricultural research should be fully cognizant of the social returns to such activity rather than focus exclusively on the returns that can be appropriated by individual states. While further empirical research is required to establish if this result is applicable to other countries as well, the potential implications for the interaction between agricultural research and investments in other public goods and education, particularly with regard to the transferability of agricultural technology, has potentially important implications that warrant further analytical and policy attention.

APPENDIX

Table A2.1:   *Composition of Output by State, 1949 and 1985*

State	Field Crops		Livestock		Fruit		Vegetables		Other	
	1949	1985	1949	1985	1949	1985	1949	1985	1949	1985
AL	39.6	32.1	56.7	61.4	1.6	0.4	0.2	0.4	1.9	5.7
AZ	54.0	35.4	27.5	42.0	3.4	10.8	13.5	7.3	1.6	4.5
AR	60.7	43.6	36.8	55.4	1.8	0.3	0.3	0.2	0.4	0.5
CA	29.8	22.3	38.9	33.0	16.6	13.3	10.6	20.0	4.1	11.3
CO	47.7	42.7	47.4	50.9	0.8	2.8	2.3	0.7	1.8	3.0
CT	11.3	7.3	62.6	57.9	2.9	0.0	1.9	2.8	21.3	32.0
DE	24.9	22.3	69.2	72.2	0.6	1.7	2.5	0.4	2.9	3.5
FL	7.1	16.6	25.7	21.0	46.3	12.0	8.0	30.5	11.2	20.0
GA	29.9	35.6	56.0	52.4	3.1	0.2	0.1	2.6	10.8	9.2
ID	56.9	58.4	41.2	37.7	0.7	1.2	0.5	1.5	0.7	1.3
IL	54.5	76.2	43.2	23.2	0.4	0.0	0.4	0.2	1.5	0.5
IN	48.2	64.0	48.7	33.6	0.5	0.4	0.9	0.2	1.8	1.8
IA	41.4	58.3	58.1	41.2	0.0	0.0	0.0	0.0	0.4	0.5
KS	63.8	57.9	35.7	41.5	0.1	0.0	0.0	0.1	0.4	0.5
KY	23.1	38.6	45.0	32.6	0.4	0.0	0.0	0.1	31.5	28.7
LA	55.4	71.0	40.4	25.3	2.6	0.1	0.2	0.8	1.2	3.1
ME	32.3	34.9	63.7	58.1	2.4	0.0	0.4	4.3	1.2	2.8
MD	25.5	26.7	60.4	59.4	1.5	1.3	2.6	0.7	10.1	12.0
MA	13.0	13.1	62.4	40.8	4.8	1.5	2.6	5.9	17.3	38.7
MI	35.3	46.6	50.3	38.4	7.9	3.4	3.1	5.8	3.4	5.8
MN	42.6	55.0	56.2	43.7	0.0	0.5	0.3	0.1	0.9	0.7
MS	55.2	56.3	43.2	42.9	1.0	0.0	0.0	0.0	0.5	0.8
MO	44.1	56.1	54.4	42.3	0.4	0.0	0.1	0.2	1.1	1.3
MT	53.7	46.5	45.7	52.7	0.2	0.0	0.0	0.3	0.5	0.5
NE	53.3	57.3	46.4	42.5	0.0	0.0	0.0	0.0	0.2	0.2
NV	29.6	48.4	69.1	51.4	0.0	0.0	0.8	0.0	0.5	0.2
NH	16.4	17.4	74.6	61.6	4.9	0.0	0.0	9.3	4.2	11.7
NJ	15.6	23.8	59.3	23.6	6.7	8.2	7.2	9.2	11.1	35.2
NM	42.1	32.7	53.8	58.2	1.9	2.8	1.7	3.2	0.5	3.1
NY	22.4	23.8	63.3	61.8	5.9	3.8	3.5	4.2	4.9	6.4
NC	22.0	21.2	30.4	48.5	1.0	0.6	0.2	0.6	46.5	29.0
ND	70.6	75.0	29.2	24.4	0.0	0.0	0.0	0.0	0.2	0.6
OH	43.6	59.4	49.1	34.2	1.2	1.5	1.5	0.6	4.6	4.3
OK	52.8	41.5	44.3	56.1	1.8	0.0	0.1	0.3	1.0	2.1
OR	36.2	40.7	47.2	36.3	7.6	5.7	4.9	7.3	4.1	10.1
PA	25.6	25.9	62.4	62.4	2.7	0.6	1.0	2.3	8.4	8.8
RI	21.6	9.1	60.3	22.8	1.7	0.0	0.8	1.6	15.5	66.5
SC	38.8	34.7	31.2	39.0	3.5	2.6	1.0	4.7	25.4	19.1
SD	46.1	49.7	53.7	49.9	0.0	0.0	0.0	0.0	0.3	0.4
TN	37.2	39.4	48.0	41.9	0.8	1.3	0.6	0.1	13.5	17.4
TX	54.6	42.6	41.6	50.3	1.3	1.2	1.6	0.7	0.9	5.0
UT	33.0	33.5	63.4	60.8	1.7	0.5	0.9	2.7	1.1	2.5
VT	22.5	17.5	75.1	79.8	1.8	0.0	0.0	1.8	0.6	0.8
VA	28.5	27.2	49.9	58.3	4.3	0.8	0.7	2.2	16.7	11.6
WA	40.5	41.5	40.0	33.4	14.9	2.2	2.7	19.0	1.9	3.8
WV	24.2	32.2	64.0	56.2	8.0	0.0	0.0	7.6	3.9	4.0
WI	27.5	31.6	69.5	65.3	0.4	1.6	1.2	0.2	1.4	1.2
WY	32.1	41.9	67.5	57.7	0.0	0.0	0.0	0.0	0.4	0.4

Table A2.2: *Composition of Input by State, 1949 and 1985.*

State	Labor 1949	Labor 1985	Land 1949	Land 1985	Capital 1949	Capital 1985	Purch. Input 1949	Purch. Input 1985
AL	51.33	25.30	16.81	7.40	10.17	19.40	21.69	47.89
AZ	12.44	6.32	35.27	35.44	9.50	9.09	42.79	49.15
AR	46.37	21.64	19.97	17.00	9.36	15.41	24.31	45.96
CA	16.59	10.52	20.42	22.40	10.22	10.97	52.77	56.11
CO	23.06	15.50	25.83	21.56	14.43	13.45	36.69	49.49
CT	22.65	21.03	7.48	3.01	21.67	24.27	48.20	51.69
DE	18.28	12.04	4.81	9.00	8.94	10.38	67.97	68.58
FL	33.56	18.35	10.98	10.58	10.45	15.60	45.01	55.47
GA	46.62	20.98	14.37	8.28	10.55	15.54	28.46	55.20
ID	23.40	14.77	31.82	29.93	13.48	13.51	31.30	41.79
IL	25.20	17.14	30.79	31.58	13.46	12.55	30.55	38.73
IN	28.28	20.61	28.21	24.06	12.79	14.40	30.72	40.93
IA	25.76	18.56	26.10	27.55	15.30	12.18	32.84	41.71
KS	27.20	18.70	31.11	21.15	15.25	14.43	26.44	45.72
KY	40.28	33.97	32.06	14.40	10.48	20.10	17.17	31.53
LA	46.16	21.33	14.27	17.02	14.49	21.08	25.08	40.56
ME	31.70	24.79	13.06	4.97	11.65	19.41	43.60	50.83
MD	26.00	19.29	9.51	9.91	16.10	17.52	48.39	53.29
MA	28.03	26.84	6.91	3.40	16.35	25.02	48.70	44.74
MI	35.56	25.11	15.68	13.82	17.62	17.40	31.14	43.67
MN	30.60	22.61	21.50	19.15	16.00	14.78	31.89	43.46
MS	52.81	23.69	19.43	14.68	8.72	18.13	19.05	43.50
MO	37.91	27.04	22.83	21.07	11.69	16.54	27.57	35.35
MT	22.78	18.88	26.50	32.35	20.04	16.14	30.68	32.63
NE	23.91	17.84	35.18	25.45	13.54	11.84	27.37	44.87
NV	6.46	4.97	65.60	65.61	12.26	9.75	15.68	19.67
NH	29.77	29.95	7.98	4.02	15.54	25.39	46.72	40.65
NJ	19.88	25.70	2.33	5.41	18.29	22.74	59.50	46.15
NM	22.67	13.14	33.83	37.12	16.68	11.97	26.82	37.77
NY	27.36	25.42	10.23	7.11	18.14	19.52	44.27	47.94
NC	50.51	26.75	14.43	6.94	11.02	15.60	24.03	50.71
ND	26.05	19.84	31.26	28.70	14.75	16.98	27.94	34.47
OH	32.49	24.99	18.35	18.49	15.40	16.44	33.76	40.08
OK	38.61	24.82	17.34	18.38	16.69	19.69	27.35	37.10
OR	24.82	17.68	28.64	36.84	13.84	13.66	32.70	31.81
PA	30.56	25.17	9.90	7.48	15.94	20.18	43.60	47.17
RI	23.41	25.71	4.95	3.09	19.56	23.12	52.09	48.07
SC	51.30	28.06	11.21	7.11	11.65	20.00	25.83	44.83
SD	29.24	22.42	20.57	23.88	18.48	15.52	31.71	38.18
TN	45.28	33.86	26.46	12.04	10.76	21.78	17.50	32.32
TX	29.93	21.13	23.82	17.52	15.34	17.49	30.92	43.86
UT	17.47	13.22	48.70	44.58	10.37	15.04	23.46	27.17
VT	30.28	24.64	9.86	5.74	17.24	21.52	42.61	48.10
VA	39.14	29.07	16.52	9.45	14.79	20.16	29.55	41.32
WA	24.73	16.21	28.99	25.35	13.92	18.19	32.35	40.25
WV	47.87	37.46	15.24	6.30	13.06	27.99	23.84	28.25
WI	30.14	26.30	19.51	11.54	18.19	18.27	32.15	43.89
WY	17.26	15.11	33.84	37.51	19.53	16.40	29.38	30.98

Table A2.3:   *Details Concerning Variables Used in Construction of Input Quantity Indexes.*

Inputs	Notes
Labor	
Operator	Adjusted for days worked-off farm. Age classes: 25-34, 35-44, 45-54, 55-64, ≥65. Education classes: 0-7 elem., 8 elem., 1-3 hsch., 4 hsch., 1-3 coll., ≥4 coll.
Unpaid family labor	Valued at the hired labor wage rate.
Hired labor	Valued at the hired labor wage rate.
Land	
Nonirrigated cropland	Excludes non-grazed forest and woodlands in farms.
Irrigated cropland	As defined by USDA
Range and Pastureland	As defined by USDA
Capital	
Autos	45% for farm use.
Trucks	85% for farm use.
Tractors	Disaggregated into 21 tractor types based on horsepower ratings.
Combines	Disaggregated into 8 performance categories listed by FIEI.
Forage equipment	Includes mower conditioners and pickup balers.
Buildings	Excludes residential structures.
Biological	Livestock inventories treated as part of farm capital only when the animals in question remain on the farm for more than one year, i.e., when they are appropriately thought of as *durable* inputs. Inventories of nonbreeder livestock of all types on farms at the beginning of year *t* are actually part of the production of year *t*-1, their initial weight is netted out of year *t*'s reported live weight production.
Dairy and beef cows	Feeder cows carried out of year *t* are part of the year *t*'s production.
Sheep	Includes only ewes over one year of age.
Sows	Average number of sows farrowing.
Other	
Fertilizer	Elemental nutrients of nitrogen, phosphorus, and potash used.
Pesti-, herbi-, and fungicides	Implicit quantities derived from preaggregated (state-level) value data using a (national-level) Divisia price index.
Purchased seed	USDA data excludes seed grown and used on farms and seed purchased for resale. Implicit quantities derived from preaggregated (state-level) value data using a national-level Divisia index that includes 12 prices.
Purchased feed	USDA data excludes feed grains or hay used on farm where grown. Implicit quantities derived from preaggregated (state-level) value data using a (national-level) Divisia index that includes 14 prices.
Fuel and oils	Implicit quantities derived from preaggregrate (state-level) value data using a (national-level) Divisia price index that includes petrol, diesel, liquid petroleum and natural gas prices.
Repairs	USDA data
Machine hire	USDA data
Electricity	Implicit quantities derived from preaggregated (state-level) value data using (state-level) price data.
Miscellaneous	Includes fencing, veterinary services, cotton ginning, insurance costs etc.

Table A2.4:   *Coefficient of Variation for Prices of Different Commodities Across States.*

Group	Commodity	1950	1960	1970	1980	1985
Field	Barley	0.251	0.362	0.348	0.557	0.797
crops	Corn	0.123	0.341	0.463	0.428	0.425
	Cotton	0.515	0.239	0.242	0.434	0.438
	Flax	0.097	0.981	1.245	1.884	2.229
	Hay	0.236	0.220	0.226	0.191	0.224
	Oats	0.151	0.343	0.407	0.600	0.659
	Peanuts	0.156	0.650	0.575	0.607	0.718
	Potato	0.230	0.269	0.418	0.603	0.776
	Rice	0.496	0.054	0.036	0.059	0.113
	Rye	0.224	0.487	0.424	0.575	0.631
	Sugarcane m.	0.867	0.874	0.885	0.185	0.167
	Sorghum	0.781	0.332	0.320	0.232	0.526
	Soybean	0.203	0.191	0.188	0.190	0.269
	Sugarbeet	1.320	0.402	0.732	0.729	1.032
	Wheat	0.229	0.162	0.064	0.171	0.064
Livestock	Broiler	0.066	0.095	0.372	0.737	0.840
	Cattle	0.093	0.102	0.082	0.064	0.103
	Eggs	0.194	0.212	0.187	0.196	0.271
	Hogs	0.047	0.044	0.068	0.048	0.052
	Milk	0.261	0.228	0.142	0.057	0.071
	Sheep	0.158	0.128	0.126	0.468	0.483
	Turkey	0.131	0.107	0.468	0.776	0.887
	Wool	0.101	0.111	0.135	0.466	0.489
Fruit	Apple	0.317	0.298	0.395	0.371	0.391
	Apricot	0.307	0.176	0.120	0.147	0.451
	Cherries	0.288	0.403	0.381	0.387	0.495
	Grapefruit	0.232	0.152	0.192	0.247	0.692
	Grapes	0.573	0.477	0.885	1.700	1.310
	Lemons	1.414	0.338	0.013	0.003	0.304
	Oranges	0.263	0.235	0.631	0.600	0.915
	Peaches	0.238	0.273	1.378	0.482	0.745
	Pears	0.343	0.610	1.499	1.680	1.622
	Pecans	0.472	0.325	0.325	0.331	0.376
	Strawberry	0.143	0.429	0.651	1.258	1.267
Vegeta-	Beans	0.325	0.748	0.789	0.745	1.180
bles	Carrot	0.622	0.841	0.974	1.045	1.061
	Cauliflower	0.532	0.333	1.187	1.176	1.137
	Celery	0.222	0.734	1.176	1.320	1.318
	Cucumbers	0.533	1.122	1.126	0.912	0.923
	Lettuce	0.591	0.501	0.781	1.194	1.152
	Onion	0.455	0.411	0.905	0.942	1.091
	Peas	0.145	0.994	1.535	1.555	1.700
	Sweet Corn fresh	0.352	0.220	0.733	0.806	0.815
	Sweet Corn proc.	0.169	0.693	1.036	0.965	1.033
	Tomato fresh	0.370	0.401	0.629	0.920	0.904
	Tomato proc	0.310	0.668	0.872	1.212	1.213
Other	Honey	0.377	0.379	0.424	0.277	0.266
	Tobacco	0.358	0.612	1.003	1.013	1.242
	Horticulture			0.078	0.061	0.034

Table A2.5:   *Value share of Land Input, All States, 1949 and 1985.*

State	Grassland		Irrigated Land		Cropland	
	1949	1985	1949	1985	1949	1985
AL	3.72	17.63	0.00	1.25	96.27	81.12
AZ	42.87	74.10	57.13	25.90	0.00	0.00
AR	5.02	13.61	4.15	20.72	90.82	65.67
CA	18.78	27.77	67.68	64.33	13.55	7.90
CO	20.71	16.20	52.31	42.30	26.99	41.50
CT	6.76	13.63	1.51	2.71	91.72	83.65
DE	2.27	1.67	0.07	10.42	97.66	87.90
FL	24.21	46.31	8.33	18.88	67.46	34.81
GA	2.75	21.02	0.03	8.61	97.22	70.37
ID	22.52	39.99	48.43	47.57	29.04	12.44
IL	2.77	2.45	0.01	0.80	97.22	96.75
IN	2.53	3.80	0.04	1.48	97.44	94.72
IA	5.74	2.94	0.01	0.31	94.26	96.76
KS	13.87	13.15	0.87	13.15	85.26	73.70
KY	3.09	11.45	0.00	0.34	96.90	88.21
LA	9.96	14.68	9.18	10.36	80.86	74.96
ME	3.07	6.19	0.16	0.85	96.78	92.95
MD	7.16	6.28	0.03	2.60	92.81	91.13
MA	3.31	10.94	2.87	6.70	93.83	82.36
MI	2.43	9.03	0.12	3.74	97.45	87.23
MN	3.93	2.43	0.02	1.58	96.06	96.00
MS	4.49	15.44	0.05	6.45	95.46	78.11
MO	8.40	11.48	0.01	2.30	91.59	86.23
MT	32.31	40.81	17.54	17.34	50.15	41.84
NE	19.16	15.95	7.07	36.54	73.77	47.51
NV	60.54	87.31	39.46	12.69	0.00	0.00
NH	4.38	16.39	0.13	0.68	95.49	82.93
NJ	9.95	1.55	2.32	14.06	87.73	84.40
NM	46.07	83.55	37.39	12.17	16.54	4.28
NY	9.99	5.27	0.20	0.87	89.81	93.85
NC	4.71	9.36	0.03	1.18	95.27	89.46
ND	8.66	10.28	0.12	0.59	91.22	89.13
OH	7.78	4.01	0.04	0.25	92.18	95.74
OK	17.01	36.24	0.50	2.88	82.49	60.88
OR	20.44	60.73	36.78	21.65	42.78	17.62
PA	7.26	7.79	0.09	0.37	92.66	91.84
RI	8.64	6.43	1.86	7.53	89.51	86.04
SC	2.48	7.39	0.12	5.10	97.41	87.52
SD	26.68	25.21	0.29	1.63	73.03	73.16
TN	4.75	8.62	0.01	0.28	95.24	91.10
TX	25.60	52.77	16.51	11.70	57.90	35.54
UT	66.72	84.03	25.74	10.93	7.54	5.04
VT	10.49	21.94	0.02	0.13	89.49	77.93
VA	10.08	19.95	0.04	0.79	89.87	79.26
WA	11.49	29.55	13.80	23.64	74.71	46.81
WV	14.63	17.11	0.00	0.05	85.37	82.84
WI	4.16	7.38	0.07	2.27	95.76	90.36
WY	54.61	67.91	39.31	24.39	6.08	7.69

Table A2.6: *Törnqvist-Theil Output Quantity Index (1980 = 1.00), Five Year Intervals, and Average Annual Growth Rate 1949-85.*

State	1949	1955	1960	1965	1970	1975	1985	Growth
CT	1.26	1.34	1.20	1.16	1.05	0.96	1.15	-0.32
ME	0.73	0.82	0.89	0.94	1.04	0.96	0.96	0.69
MA	1.40	1.42	1.20	1.11	0.95	0.92	1.01	-0.83
NH	1.25	1.41	1.20	1.15	1.02	1.00	1.03	-0.60
RI	1.23	1.24	1.22	1.13	0.99	0.98	1.80	0.79
VT	0.94	1.00	0.97	0.94	0.93	0.89	1.04	0.31
DE	0.44	0.50	0.67	0.76	0.85	0.91	1.38	2.93
MD	0.55	0.60	0.71	0.79	0.85	0.91	1.30	2.30
NJ	1.65	1.86	1.83	1.60	1.22	0.96	1.35	-0.82
NY	0.83	0.92	0.89	0.90	0.90	0.89	1.04	0.53
PA	0.71	0.76	0.79	0.79	0.82	0.84	1.24	1.46
IL	0.63	0.70	0.76	0.86	0.79	1.03	1.18	1.58
IN	0.61	0.68	0.74	0.78	0.76	0.88	1.12	1.57
IA	0.54	0.60	0.67	0.71	0.78	0.79	1.00	1.54
MO	0.73	0.76	0.81	0.86	0.91	0.95	1.15	1.09
OH	0.69	0.73	0.72	0.71	0.73	0.86	1.13	1.29
MI	0.71	0.71	0.70	0.73	0.73	0.81	1.19	1.37
MN	0.54	0.63	0.69	0.68	0.75	0.78	1.11	1.97
WI	0.65	0.74	0.74	0.77	0.80	0.81	1.06	1.33
KS	0.48	0.46	0.74	0.70	0.84	0.90	1.16	2.15
NE	0.44	0.47	0.63	0.64	0.77	0.85	1.24	2.49
ND	0.72	0.93	0.92	1.16	1.06	1.31	1.65	2.05
SD	0.56	0.68	0.81	0.87	0.96	0.83	1.24	2.09
KY	0.82	0.74	0.77	0.87	0.87	0.96	1.10	0.99
NC	0.60	0.72	0.75	0.76	0.88	0.95	1.04	1.50
TN	0.79	0.79	0.79	0.85	0.84	0.93	1.25	1.34
VA	0.85	0.85	0.88	0.84	0.88	0.94	1.15	0.87
WV	1.27	1.25	1.12	0.93	0.91	0.95	1.01	-0.52
AL	0.55	0.67	0.68	0.82	0.87	1.03	1.18	2.35
FL	0.26	0.41	0.41	0.53	0.61	0.84	0.93	3.40
GA	0.41	0.53	0.62	0.74	0.88	1.02	1.21	3.08
SC	0.83	0.96	0.86	0.93	0.93	1.12	1.10	0.99
AR	0.42	0.48	0.51	0.67	0.80	0.96	1.21	3.07
LA	0.56	0.65	0.60	0.74	0.90	0.94	1.08	2.08
MS	0.62	0.83	0.77	0.99	1.09	1.00	1.20	1.85
OK	0.63	0.49	0.68	0.72	0.78	0.90	1.00	1.57
TX	0.68	0.57	0.68	0.75	0.85	0.98	1.15	1.73
AZ	0.37	0.49	0.59	0.67	0.73	0.80	1.00	2.80
CO	0.51	0.44	0.63	0.59	0.84	0.90	1.09	2.12
ID	0.40	0.52	0.55	0.67	0.75	0.81	1.04	2.56
MT	0.57	0.85	0.73	0.88	0.94	1.06	0.74	0.94
NV	0.63	0.63	0.66	0.75	0.85	0.87	1.07	1.60
NM	0.57	0.56	0.66	0.66	0.86	0.86	1.23	2.17
UT	0.74	0.84	0.81	0.85	0.96	0.94	1.07	1.00
WY	0.66	0.74	0.78	0.86	0.91	0.99	0.94	0.93
CA	0.40	0.51	0.58	0.65	0.69	0.86	1.08	2.66
OR	0.55	0.61	0.63	0.68	0.72	0.81	1.07	1.87
WA	0.44	0.48	0.50	0.58	0.64	0.83	1.03	2.44

Table A 2.7:   *Törnqvist-Theil Input Quantity Index (1980 = 1.00), Five Year Intervals, and Average Annual Growth Rate 1949-85.*

State	1949	1955	1960	1965	1970	1975	1985	Growth
CT	1.50	1.40	1.31	1.11	1.00	0.85	1.01	-1.04
ME	1.15	1.05	1.10	1.01	0.96	0.87	0.83	-0.82
MA	1.88	1.61	1.44	1.16	0.98	0.89	1.11	-1.40
NH	1.74	1.46	1.29	1.02	0.97	0.92	1.04	-1.31
RI	1.99	1.70	1.70	1.35	1.01	0.90	1.01	-1.77
VT	1.01	0.97	0.96	0.85	0.84	0.83	1.03	0.08
DE	0.70	0.71	0.78	0.78	0.80	0.70	1.09	1.23
MD	0.69	0.72	0.76	0.78	0.80	0.76	1.03	1.11
NJ	1.61	1.68	1.47	1.16	0.98	0.90	1.02	-1.25
NY	1.07	1.07	1.05	0.98	0.94	0.93	0.96	-0.23
PA	0.89	0.93	0.92	0.84	0.82	0.82	1.02	0.39
IL	0.71	0.79	0.82	0.85	0.91	0.92	0.93	0.74
IN	0.74	0.82	0.84	0.83	0.87	0.88	0.94	0.66
IA	0.68	0.77	0.80	0.83	0.91	0.91	0.92	0.85
MO	0.79	0.84	0.86	0.88	0.94	0.91	0.93	0.43
OH	0.87	0.90	0.88	0.86	0.89	0.89	0.92	0.21
MI	0.93	0.98	0.96	0.91	0.86	0.85	1.02	0.27
MN	0.72	0.80	0.85	0.84	0.84	0.87	0.98	0.83
WI	0.77	0.82	0.83	0.81	0.81	0.84	1.01	0.77
KS	0.68	0.73	0.75	0.78	0.86	0.82	0.96	0.90
NE	0.62	0.70	0.73	0.77	0.84	0.85	0.96	1.17
ND	0.75	0.84	0.84	0.86	0.88	0.94	0.97	0.69
SD	0.79	0.87	0.90	0.92	0.95	0.95	0.99	0.64
KY	1.02	0.96	0.92	0.92	0.91	0.87	0.97	-0.15
NC	1.01	1.05	0.98	0.94	0.92	0.85	0.95	-0.16
TN	1.10	1.05	0.99	0.98	0.97	0.91	1.00	-0.26
VA	0.96	0.98	0.91	0.86	0.83	0.82	0.98	0.04
WV	1.64	1.45	1.20	1.03	0.86	0.86	0.94	-1.43
AL	1.05	0.98	0.92	0.93	0.98	0.89	0.93	-0.34
FL	0.36	0.48	0.58	0.61	0.72	0.75	0.95	2.58
GA	0.81	0.82	0.82	0.83	0.92	0.84	0.91	0.30
SC	1.41	1.31	1.14	1.01	0.94	0.90	0.88	-1.22
AR	0.79	0.76	0.74	0.83	0.91	0.83	0.97	0.54
LA	0.88	0.91	0.85	0.88	0.90	0.86	0.94	0.17
MS	1.30	1.25	1.10	1.07	1.05	0.94	0.91	-0.94
OK	0.79	0.74	0.72	0.79	0.85	0.82	0.88	0.33
TX	0.71	0.72	0.74	0.82	0.91	0.85	0.97	0.85
AZ	0.41	0.55	0.69	0.75	0.85	0.86	0.95	2.23
CO	0.61	0.64	0.71	0.76	0.86	0.81	0.98	1.32
ID	0.62	0.71	0.76	0.79	0.82	0.84	0.99	1.23
MT	0.74	0.83	0.86	0.88	0.93	0.91	1.01	0.83
NV	0.74	0.66	0.72	0.78	0.83	0.84	0.98	0.74
NM	0.66	0.70	0.72	0.82	0.87	0.85	0.98	1.01
UT	0.93	0.86	0.88	0.88	0.87	0.85	0.98	0.17
WY	0.77	0.77	0.81	0.83	0.88	0.88	1.00	0.72
CA	0.55	0.64	0.74	0.78	0.81	0.82	1.01	1.61
OR	0.76	0.81	0.80	0.81	0.80	0.82	0.99	0.71
WA	0.52	0.56	0.60	0.63	0.63	0.89	0.98	1.77

Table A2.8: *Törnqvist-Theil Labor Quantity Index (1980 = 1.00), Five Year Intervals, and Average Annual Growth Rate 1949-85.*

State	1949	1955	1960	1965	1970	1975	1985	Growth
CT	4.24	2.87	2.05	1.61	1.19	1.00	0.95	-3.83
ME	4.03	2.62	2.02	1.54	1.10	0.98	0.91	-3.81
MA	5.03	3.10	2.22	1.68	1.18	0.96	1.13	-3.84
NH	4.22	2.59	1.77	1.32	0.95	0.92	0.99	-3.72
RI	4.14	2.68	2.07	1.63	1.05	0.93	0.93	-3.81
VT	2.84	2.03	1.60	1.28	1.03	0.97	0.97	-2.75
DE	2.38	1.79	1.50	1.27	1.04	1.01	0.94	-2.39
MD	2.08	1.70	1.38	1.19	1.01	0.98	0.97	-1.98
NJ	3.14	2.58	1.86	1.37	1.03	0.97	1.04	-2.92
NY	2.62	1.97	1.59	1.33	1.09	1.08	0.94	-2.66
PA	2.38	1.88	1.53	1.30	1.03	1.02	1.00	-2.27
IL	1.97	1.71	1.48	1.31	1.17	1.10	0.92	-2.01
IN	2.12	1.75	1.44	1.23	1.10	1.06	0.95	-2.10
IA	1.77	1.63	1.44	1.30	1.17	1.09	0.92	-1.72
MO	2.25	1.78	1.45	1.28	1.15	1.06	0.97	-2.22
OH	2.37	1.85	1.48	1.29	1.13	1.06	0.97	-2.33
MI	2.60	2.00	1.63	1.33	1.08	1.03	0.98	-2.52
MN	1.80	1.59	1.40	1.26	1.06	1.03	0.95	-1.68
WI	1.82	1.56	1.33	1.19	1.02	1.03	0.98	-1.62
KS	1.97	1.65	1.41	1.28	1.16	1.07	0.95	-1.91
NE	1.73	1.58	1.40	1.25	1.12	1.07	0.98	-1.53
ND	1.62	1.51	1.34	1.22	1.13	1.07	0.96	-1.39
SD	1.69	1.58	1.41	1.28	1.17	1.10	0.98	-1.47
KY	2.60	2.09	1.63	1.43	1.20	1.06	0.98	-2.55
NC	3.53	3.01	2.21	1.73	1.31	1.17	0.85	-3.73
TN	3.02	2.36	1.78	1.51	1.24	1.08	0.99	-2.94
VA	2.83	2.25	1.68	1.42	1.11	1.04	0.95	-2.83
WV	4.60	3.33	2.19	1.68	1.16	1.05	1.04	-3.88
AL	4.67	3.31	2.24	1.71	1.29	1.17	0.96	-4.16
FL	1.57	1.38	1.14	1.03	0.90	0.93	1.03	-1.10
GA	4.14	2.87	1.90	1.45	1.18	1.12	0.91	-3.92
SC	5.24	3.99	2.64	1.82	1.25	1.16	0.90	-4.59
AR	3.66	2.49	1.70	1.36	1.07	1.05	1.02	-3.38
LA	3.55	2.72	1.88	1.51	1.13	1.08	0.94	-3.47
MS	5.92	4.49	2.87	2.06	1.36	1.24	0.90	-4.91
OK	2.53	1.75	1.39	1.29	1.17	1.07	0.99	-2.43
TX	2.36	1.74	1.33	1.26	1.20	1.05	1.05	-2.11
AZ	1.70	1.35	1.10	1.01	0.93	0.93	1.07	-1.16
CO	1.81	1.53	1.28	1.18	1.08	1.02	1.00	-1.59
ID	1.75	1.59	1.38	1.20	1.06	1.03	1.00	-1.49
MT	1.51	1.38	1.25	1.18	1.08	1.01	1.03	-1.02
NV	1.35	1.18	1.02	0.99	0.94	0.89	1.12	-0.52
NM	2.22	1.72	1.35	1.19	0.98	0.94	1.07	-1.88
UT	2.22	1.74	1.44	1.23	1.04	0.99	1.02	-2.03
WY	1.60	1.39	1.20	1.17	1.10	1.00	1.04	-1.15
CA	1.89	1.57	1.30	1.10	0.99	0.91	1.08	-1.50
OR	1.84	1.53	1.21	1.08	0.87	0.91	1.06	-1.45
WA	1.88	1.53	1.29	1.14	0.94	0.94	1.01	-1.59

Table A2.9:   *Törnqvist-Theil Land Quantity Index (1980 = 1.00), Five Year Intervals, and Average Annual Growth Rate 1949-85.*

State	1949	1955	1960	1965	1970	1975	1985	Growth
CT	2.21	1.97	1.60	1.31	1.04	0.98	0.89	-2.37
ME	2.23	1.96	1.67	1.38	1.10	1.03	0.85	-2.49
MA	2.25	1.93	1.59	1.22	0.97	0.95	0.85	-2.54
NH	2.63	2.15	1.70	1.37	1.08	1.00	0.79	-3.11
RI	2.57	2.12	1.84	1.35	1.01	0.98	0.74	-3.20
VT	1.59	1.45	1.32	1.13	1.04	0.98	0.94	-1.37
DE	1.03	0.99	0.96	0.96	0.97	0.94	0.97	-0.16
MD	1.30	1.23	1.20	1.13	1.02	0.98	0.97	-0.76
NJ	1.60	1.52	1.38	1.16	1.01	0.99	0.85	-1.63
NY	1.53	1.41	1.32	1.18	1.03	1.02	0.88	-1.43
PA	1.44	1.31	1.22	1.09	0.97	0.96	0.95	-1.08
IL	0.97	0.96	0.98	0.98	1.00	0.98	0.97	0.04
IN	1.03	1.02	1.02	1.01	1.01	0.99	0.97	-0.14
IA	0.96	0.96	0.99	0.97	0.99	0.99	0.98	0.05
MO	0.95	0.92	0.95	0.95	1.01	0.99	0.94	0.02
OH	1.16	1.10	1.07	1.06	1.04	0.99	0.96	-0.49
MI	1.26	1.21	1.15	1.09	0.98	0.95	1.01	-0.60
MN	1.02	1.01	1.01	1.02	1.00	0.97	0.98	-0.11
WI	1.09	1.07	1.05	1.03	0.98	0.99	0.96	-0.34
KS	0.94	0.96	0.97	0.98	1.01	0.99	0.99	0.14
NE	0.86	0.85	0.88	0.88	0.90	0.94	1.01	0.44
ND	0.99	1.00	1.00	1.00	1.03	1.02	0.97	-0.05
SD	1.04	1.04	1.04	1.02	1.03	1.02	0.99	-0.14
KY	1.26	1.13	1.10	1.03	1.02	0.98	0.95	-0.71
NC	1.26	1.17	1.08	1.01	0.99	0.97	0.96	-0.70
TN	1.28	1.17	1.12	1.06	1.10	1.02	0.94	-0.79
VA	1.29	1.13	1.09	1.01	1.03	0.98	0.97	-0.72
WV	1.98	1.56	1.37	1.10	1.11	1.00	0.84	-2.18
AL	1.58	1.35	1.15	1.04	1.10	1.06	0.89	-1.46
FL	0.71	0.85	1.01	0.98	0.95	0.96	0.99	0.89
GA	1.50	1.27	1.11	0.96	0.98	0.98	0.99	-1.06
SC	1.61	1.43	1.25	1.16	1.09	1.01	0.88	-1.55
AR	0.91	0.86	0.86	0.87	0.98	0.96	0.99	0.23
LA	0.93	0.91	0.85	0.89	0.96	0.94	0.94	0.06
MS	1.12	1.00	0.92	0.91	1.03	1.02	0.94	-0.45
OK	0.99	0.95	0.92	0.95	1.02	0.99	0.99	0.01
TX	0.85	0.91	0.94	0.96	1.00	0.98	0.98	0.36
AZ	0.94	1.03	1.00	0.98	1.00	0.98	0.96	0.05
CO	0.98	0.90	0.93	0.93	0.95	0.95	0.96	-0.03
ID	0.86	0.91	0.92	0.95	0.95	0.95	0.97	0.33
MT	0.93	0.97	0.97	0.98	0.99	0.97	1.00	0.18
NV	1.11	0.90	0.94	1.04	1.01	0.99	0.99	-0.25
NM	0.97	0.93	0.95	1.00	0.99	0.99	0.97	0.02
UT	1.33	1.11	1.05	1.08	1.03	0.99	0.97	-0.81
WY	1.00	0.96	0.98	0.99	0.98	0.97	0.98	-0.03
CA	0.97	0.99	0.97	0.96	0.93	0.96	0.98	0.02
OR	1.00	1.01	0.99	1.00	0.98	1.00	0.96	-0.11
WA	0.87	0.89	0.93	0.96	0.95	0.94	1.02	0.41

Table A2.10:   *Törnqvist-Theil Capital Quantity Index (1980 = 1.00), Five Year Intervals, and Average Annual Growth Rate 1949-85.*

State	1949	1955	1960	1965	1970	1975	1985	Growth
CT	0.90	0.84	0.79	0.67	0.62	0.72	1.26	0.78
ME	0.64	0.69	0.71	0.65	0.63	0.77	1.19	1.59
MA	0.73	0.72	0.67	0.58	0.52	0.67	1.32	1.46
NH	0.76	0.75	0.67	0.59	0.60	0.76	1.32	1.37
RI	1.04	1.08	0.89	0.74	0.55	0.71	1.16	0.16
VT	0.55	0.61	0.63	0.63	0.70	0.86	1.17	1.95
DE	0.36	0.50	0.57	0.56	0.56	0.79	0.92	2.61
MD	0.33	0.46	0.50	0.55	0.57	0.72	0.97	2.88
NJ	0.70	0.70	0.67	0.59	0.52	0.67	1.11	1.14
NY	0.63	0.77	0.81	0.81	0.79	0.96	1.05	1.39
PA	0.40	0.52	0.57	0.57	0.59	0.74	1.01	2.54
IL	0.37	0.56	0.60	0.67	0.75	0.86	0.80	2.19
IN	0.32	0.49	0.52	0.56	0.62	0.76	0.79	2.50
IA	0.39	0.57	0.54	0.58	0.61	0.75	0.75	1.91
MO	0.30	0.49	0.52	0.59	0.62	0.78	0.87	2.94
OH	0.37	0.52	0.54	0.58	0.63	0.76	0.78	2.07
MI	0.50	0.70	0.73	0.75	0.71	0.80	0.97	1.83
MN	0.39	0.59	0.67	0.69	0.66	0.78	0.87	2.27
WI	0.42	0.56	0.61	0.63	0.62	0.73	0.92	2.20
KS	0.50	0.71	0.68	0.74	0.72	0.84	0.92	1.70
NE	0.45	0.65	0.65	0.71	0.69	0.84	0.87	1.91
ND	0.41	0.67	0.69	0.77	0.77	0.92	0.98	2.42
SD	0.50	0.71	0.74	0.80	0.77	0.92	0.98	1.88
KY	0.30	0.36	0.43	0.54	0.58	0.70	0.97	3.24
NC	0.36	0.54	0.57	0.64	0.64	0.75	0.96	2.62
TN	0.30	0.42	0.48	0.55	0.58	0.71	1.02	3.24
VA	0.39	0.51	0.50	0.53	0.56	0.72	1.04	2.62
WV	0.40	0.51	0.49	0.51	0.50	0.75	0.85	2.09
AL	0.33	0.45	0.48	0.55	0.63	0.81	0.92	2.76
FL	0.17	0.28	0.35	0.43	0.50	0.77	1.03	4.89
GA	0.34	0.48	0.53	0.56	0.63	0.81	0.93	2.68
SC	0.46	0.59	0.62	0.64	0.66	0.83	0.87	1.75
AR	0.29	0.44	0.45	0.59	0.65	0.78	0.95	3.18
LA	0.38	0.52	0.57	0.68	0.70	0.78	0.94	2.46
MS	0.37	0.60	0.65	0.73	0.76	0.84	0.89	2.37
OK	0.41	0.45	0.46	0.55	0.59	0.79	0.94	2.39
TX	0.50	0.60	0.56	0.65	0.71	0.85	1.25	2.39
AZ	0.21	0.31	0.36	0.40	0.47	0.63	1.04	4.40
CO	0.41	0.56	0.59	0.65	0.65	0.76	1.10	2.67
ID	0.35	0.53	0.55	0.59	0.61	0.76	1.07	3.05
MT	0.49	0.66	0.68	0.76	0.78	0.89	1.06	2.13
NV	0.33	0.32	0.31	0.35	0.44	0.64	0.87	2.77
NM	0.39	0.48	0.44	0.51	0.54	0.69	0.97	2.49
UT	0.32	0.40	0.44	0.46	0.48	0.60	0.97	3.10
WY	0.46	0.49	0.52	0.58	0.62	0.85	1.02	2.23
CA	0.30	0.42	0.49	0.55	0.54	0.65	1.14	3.65
OR	0.32	0.47	0.43	0.49	0.52	0.64	1.03	3.18
WA	0.23	0.34	0.35	0.35	0.37	1.24	0.86	3.55

Table A2.11:   *Törnqvist-Theil Purchased Input Quantity Index (1980 = 1.00),*
                 Five Year Intervals, and Average Annual Growth Rate 1949-85.

State	1949	1955	1960	1965	1970	1975	1985	Growth
CT	1.14	1.21	1.28	1.12	1.09	0.85	0.96	-0.44
ME	0.64	0.70	0.89	0.91	0.99	0.85	0.73	0.40
MA	1.59	1.53	1.52	1.23	1.14	0.97	1.04	-1.13
NH	1.41	1.33	1.36	1.07	1.16	0.98	0.98	-0.85
RI	1.77	1.58	1.89	1.50	1.21	0.96	1.02	-1.42
VT	0.67	0.74	0.83	0.75	0.81	0.76	1.01	1.18
DE	0.55	0.58	0.68	0.71	0.78	0.61	1.16	2.03
MD	0.48	0.52	0.63	0.70	0.79	0.68	1.08	2.23
NJ	1.73	1.97	1.78	1.39	1.21	0.99	1.01	-1.49
NY	0.77	0.83	0.90	0.87	0.92	0.84	0.96	0.68
PA	0.62	0.73	0.79	0.74	0.82	0.75	1.05	1.42
IL	0.37	0.49	0.56	0.65	0.81	0.83	0.94	2.52
IN	0.40	0.54	0.63	0.67	0.80	0.78	0.99	2.41
IA	0.35	0.46	0.56	0.66	0.87	0.85	0.95	2.67
MO	0.40	0.52	0.64	0.74	0.91	0.84	0.92	2.20
OH	0.52	0.63	0.69	0.70	0.83	0.82	0.94	1.66
MI	0.49	0.62	0.69	0.70	0.78	0.74	1.06	2.10
MN	0.38	0.48	0.59	0.62	0.73	0.76	1.04	2.69
WI	0.46	0.55	0.62	0.63	0.76	0.75	1.09	2.37
KS	0.29	0.35	0.43	0.51	0.71	0.66	0.96	3.21
NE	0.27	0.36	0.45	0.55	0.75	0.72	0.96	3.35
ND	0.41	0.48	0.52	0.59	0.67	0.80	0.97	2.31
SD	0.43	0.51	0.62	0.71	0.85	0.83	0.99	2.30
KY	0.40	0.47	0.57	0.66	0.80	0.75	0.96	2.35
NC	0.32	0.43	0.54	0.64	0.81	0.70	1.01	3.14
TN	0.41	0.52	0.66	0.77	0.93	0.83	1.02	2.41
VA	0.47	0.60	0.66	0.66	0.75	0.68	0.98	1.95
WV	0.89	0.97	1.00	0.94	0.88	0.75	0.96	0.23
AL	0.30	0.41	0.58	0.75	0.97	0.78	0.93	3.08
FL	0.19	0.33	0.45	0.51	0.70	0.67	0.91	4.11
GA	0.27	0.41	0.57	0.70	0.91	0.75	0.90	3.19
SC	0.49	0.57	0.67	0.73	0.86	0.77	0.89	1.67
AR	0.27	0.37	0.50	0.70	0.90	0.74	0.96	3.36
LA	0.33	0.47	0.57	0.69	0.87	0.78	0.93	2.73
MS	0.36	0.50	0.66	0.84	1.02	0.81	0.91	2.46
OK	0.34	0.39	0.47	0.59	0.73	0.66	0.78	2.24
TX	0.34	0.40	0.51	0.64	0.83	0.73	0.86	2.58
AZ	0.24	0.40	0.63	0.71	0.86	0.84	0.92	3.51
CO	0.32	0.38	0.51	0.60	0.81	0.72	0.97	3.04
ID	0.31	0.39	0.51	0.58	0.69	0.70	0.98	3.10
MT	0.46	0.55	0.66	0.69	0.86	0.80	0.97	2.04
NV	0.29	0.34	0.48	0.52	0.65	0.60	0.97	3.08
NM	0.30	0.42	0.52	0.70	0.85	0.78	0.96	2.96
UT	0.50	0.55	0.69	0.71	0.81	0.73	0.98	1.85
WY	0.50	0.56	0.66	0.69	0.84	0.77	1.00	1.77
CA	0.36	0.47	0.65	0.72	0.79	0.80	0.99	2.67
OR	0.43	0.51	0.59	0.64	0.69	0.66	0.98	2.18
WA	0.34	0.42	0.54	0.62	0.69	0.68	1.01	3.01

Table A2.12: *Total Value of the Flow of Research Services by State, Mns of Constant 1980 $ and Avg. Growth Rates 1910-85, 1950-85.*

State	1915	1925	1935	1945	1955	1965	1975	1985	1910-85*	1950-85*
CT	1.07	2.02	3.03	2.70	4.66	6.03	5.50	4.97	2.22	0.45
ME	0.86	0.79	1.24	2.10	2.42	3.16	4.59	5.83	3.06	3.00
MA	1.12	1.74	2.88	2.23	3.27	3.97	3.11	6.18	2.73	2.13
NH	0.50	0.56	1.10	0.77	1.45	1.93	1.95	1.92	2.00	2.21
RI	0.35	0.41	0.80	0.85	1.36	1.91	2.35	1.80	2.08	1.32
VT	0.47	0.49	0.93	0.83	1.30	1.79	2.79	2.88	2.47	3.01
DE	0.42	0.61	1.03	1.41	2.00	2.26	2.74	3.73	3.22	2.21
MD	0.61	1.14	1.57	1.99	3.81	5.65	6.96	8.73	3.62	3.21
NJ	1.89	1.87	4.74	5.49	6.99	9.94	9.66	10.43	2.86	1.55
NY	1.88	4.53	9.79	12.15	20.05	24.55	31.05	53.83	4.65	3.30
PA	0.94	1.08	2.29	4.19	7.71	10.55	13.28	17.28	4.34	2.89
IL	2.86	2.99	4.62	6.78	10.99	15.11	15.93	20.08	3.01	1.87
IN	3.06	3.74	5.15	6.37	11.55	11.97	19.30	25.84	3.48	2.66
IA	1.87	2.58	2.95	4.96	11.36	13.74	17.73	22.16	4.09	2.56
MO	1.46	1.20	1.98	2.84	5.43	10.95	13.77	18.45	5.23	4.48
OH	3.49	4.09	5.06	5.61	9.19	11.64	14.19	18.29	2.63	2.77
MI	0.84	2.47	3.12	3.76	10.09	14.12	19.65	27.18	5.50	3.80
MN	3.53	3.61	4.41	5.32	11.32	15.21	18.92	26.20	2.99	3.01
WI	1.62	2.77	4.09	8.24	12.85	16.03	19.70	29.51	5.52	2.96
KS	1.43	1.54	2.25	3.21	8.26	10.59	16.71	19.96	3.95	4.55
NE	1.15	1.75	2.66	3.40	6.44	11.25	19.24	20.37	4.49	3.65
ND	1.37	2.08	1.42	2.05	3.89	6.30	9.86	12.90	4.41	3.82
SD	0.48	0.94	1.01	1.61	3.07	5.54	6.43	4.84	3.01	2.12
KY	2.83	2.43	2.91	3.58	5.95	9.22	9.43	11.90	2.61	2.82
NC	1.45	0.91	1.89	3.56	9.42	14.16	26.14	38.43	6.50	4.59
TN	0.68	0.76	1.17	2.47	5.31	8.41	11.65	13.97	4.52	3.37
VA	0.63	0.95	1.52	3.01	6.73	9.89	14.95	22.72	5.22	4.84
WV	0.88	1.39	1.54	2.06	3.14	4.07	4.07	3.83	2.10	0.91
AL	0.75	0.75	1.94	4.37	7.88	11.06	15.44	18.45	4.26	2.91
FL	0.56	1.64	3.67	9.03	13.74	19.67	31.20	43.66	6.42	3.15
GA	0.42	0.45	1.09	2.72	9.43	12.77	19.90	30.44	6.02	6.34
SC	0.54	1.07	1.85	4.11	4.58	6.61	11.02	13.73	4.76	3.69
AR	0.51	0.78	1.57	2.44	4.52	10.34	12.85	15.39	3.63	3.81
LA	0.92	1.02	1.79	3.61	9.35	13.77	18.65	21.96	4.41	3.41
MS	0.55	1.35	1.95	3.68	7.25	9.28	15.63	19.66	4.45	2.92
OK	0.40	0.69	1.90	4.38	7.15	8.42	10.41	13.07	4.74	2.38
TX	1.26	3.20	5.42	7.76	14.90	15.84	27.37	46.33	5.52	3.79
AZ	0.83	1.15	1.58	1.73	3.17	8.47	10.48	14.58	4.56	5.16
CO	0.62	1.27	1.83	2.42	4.74	7.03	7.40	22.43	4.94	5.65
ID	0.40	0.70	0.98	1.20	3.47	5.05	9.31	10.30	4.36	3.88
MT	1.22	1.35	1.77	2.68	4.84	5.99	8.62	8.96	2.84	2.23
NV	0.38	0.40	0.79	0.81	0.97	2.20	3.12	3.32	2.54	4.35

Table A2.12 cont'd: *Total Value of the Flow of Research Services by State, Mns of Constant 1980 $ and Avg. Growth Rates 1910-85, 1950-85.*

State	1915	1925	1935	1945	1955	1965	1975	1985	1910-85*	1950-85*
NM	0.49	0.47	0.93	1.19	2.46	3.39	3.93	6.58	3.67	3.75
UT	0.58	0.99	1.18	1.55	3.44	3.93	5.76	8.07	3.56	3.04
WY	0.43	0.66	1.50	1.45	2.74	3.53	2.88	3.83	2.99	1.57
CA	2.31	4.92	8.34	13.74	30.60	51.08	65.85	85.79	5.84	3.78
OR	0.81	1.60	2.21	4.40	8.42	12.89	17.27	24.61	4.23	3.34
WA	1.06	1.58	1.74	4.26	10.24	12.74	21.74	20.47	4.85	2.31

Note: * = average annual growth rate.

Table A2.13:   *Research Intensity Ratios by State, Five Year Intervals, Average Annual Growth Rate 1949-85, and Rank (in 1985).*

State	1949	1955	1960	1965	1970	1975	1980	1985	Growth	Rank
CT	0.54	0.81	1.18	1.63	2.02	1.94	1.65	2.20	3.82	9
ME	0.23	0.34	0.48	0.58	0.84	0.78	1.25	2.59	6.34	5
MA	0.38	0.58	0.84	1.15	1.30	1.19	1.65	3.05	5.53	3
NH	0.27	0.59	0.91	1.45	1.91	1.83	2.42	2.47	6.13	7
RI	0.99	1.84	2.59	3.87	6.01	6.96	8.69	4.64	4.22	1
VT	0.14	0.25	0.35	0.50	0.73	0.77	0.70	0.93	5.09	31
DE	0.35	0.54	0.71	0.74	1.21	0.81	1.09	1.10	2.97	25
MD	0.22	0.39	0.53	0.68	0.83	0.75	0.74	1.02	3.97	28
NJ	0.48	0.74	0.97	1.79	2.20	2.74	3.67	3.27	5.10	2
NY	0.36	0.61	0.72	1.03	1.42	1.26	1.57	2.72	5.27	4
PA	0.14	0.24	0.33	0.46	0.57	0.54	0.47	0.73	4.16	36
IL	0.10	0.14	0.19	0.23	0.35	0.18	0.21	0.36	3.40	46
IN	0.16	0.24	0.28	0.33	0.44	0.42	0.52	0.81	4.18	33
IA	0.07	0.12	0.15	0.17	0.19	0.18	0.17	0.31	4.17	47
MO	0.06	0.12	0.23	0.32	0.42	0.34	0.39	0.62	6.27	42
OH	0.11	0.20	0.30	0.38	0.42	0.36	0.37	0.62	4.52	41
MI	0.14	0.36	0.52	0.74	0.85	0.85	0.71	1.26	5.23	22
MN	0.12	0.18	0.26	0.35	0.43	0.32	0.36	0.53	3.88	44
WI	0.17	0.26	0.36	0.44	0.51	0.43	0.45	0.70	3.72	38
KS	0.08	0.25	0.25	0.36	0.38	0.38	0.44	0.56	5.42	43
NE	0.10	0.16	0.23	0.33	0.37	0.37	0.40	0.45	4.30	45
ND	0.11	0.15	0.22	0.33	0.49	0.34	0.66	0.70	5.17	37
SD	0.07	0.12	0.18	0.26	0.32	0.27	0.23	0.22	3.27	48
KY	0.14	0.25	0.34	0.46	0.53	0.43	0.47	0.69	4.16	40
NC	0.17	0.23	0.33	0.50	0.66	0.74	0.99	1.46	5.73	17
TN	0.14	0.24	0.33	0.53	0.65	0.71	0.88	0.98	5.15	30
VA	0.16	0.33	0.49	0.73	0.91	1.04	1.42	1.84	6.62	14
WV	0.30	0.51	0.81	1.33	1.65	1.50	1.42	1.86	4.74	12
AL	0.26	0.38	0.55	0.71	0.86	0.83	1.01	1.30	3.86	21
FL	0.57	0.64	0.74	0.94	1.25	1.14	1.13	1.50	2.24	16
GA	0.11	0.35	0.45	0.58	0.75	0.69	1.04	1.39	6.60	19
SC	0.21	0.31	0.51	0.70	0.96	0.98	1.34	1.87	5.66	11
AR	0.14	0.19	0.41	0.48	0.49	0.46	0.54	0.70	4.24	39
LA	0.36	0.63	1.04	1.25	1.27	1.39	1.50	2.53	5.04	6
MS	0.27	0.29	0.45	0.50	0.72	0.89	1.13	1.45	4.55	18
OK	0.16	0.38	0.37	0.48	0.50	0.45	0.43	0.77	3.83	34
TX	0.11	0.22	0.29	0.28	0.38	0.38	0.43	0.81	5.21	32
AZ	0.24	0.30	0.67	0.91	1.08	0.97	1.09	1.63	5.16	15
CO	0.14	0.33	0.29	0.51	0.42	0.34	1.04	1.37	6.10	20
ID	0.16	0.24	0.34	0.41	0.51	0.54	0.58	0.74	3.99	35
MT	0.21	0.26	0.42	0.49	0.65	0.52	0.62	1.15	4.55	23
NV	0.28	0.52	0.92	1.49	1.58	1.53	1.45	1.85	5.15	13
NM	0.20	0.41	0.49	0.70	0.69	0.59	0.41	1.06	4.59	27

Tab. A2.13 cont.:   *Research Intensity Ratios by State, Five Year Intervals, Average Annual Growth Rate 1949-85, and Rank (in 1985).*

State	1949	1955	1960	1965	1970	1975	1980	1985	Growth	Rank
UT	0.30	0.52	0.70	0.91	0.91	1.14	1.27	1.88	4.71	10
WY	0.28	0.52	0.61	0.80	0.85	0.55	0.53	1.01	3.47	29
CA	0.27	0.37	0.56	0.68	0.76	0.70	0.74	1.08	3.71	26
OR	0.42	0.60	0.86	1.30	1.47	1.32	1.52	2.31	4.40	8
WA	0.34	0.54	0.75	0.92	1.12	0.95	0.94	1.14	2.88	24

Table A2.14: *States' Contribution to the National Research Stock Compared to their Reception of Spillins, 1949, 1985.*

State	1949			1985			
	Research	Spillins	Net Gain	Research	Spillins	Net Gain	Rank
CT	2.22	2.00	-0.22	0.98	1.97	0.98	36
ME	1.04	1.50	0.46	0.67	1.47	0.80	34
MA	1.93	2.10	0.17	0.67	2.04	1.37	40
NH	0.72	2.22	1.50	0.34	2.11	1.77	47
RI	0.56	1.89	1.33	0.36	1.79	1.43	42
VT	0.65	2.14	1.48	0.38	2.03	1.65	46
DE	0.79	0.96	0.17	0.47	1.00	0.53	30
MD	1.31	2.32	1.02	1.10	2.28	1.19	38
NJ	3.58	1.97	-1.61	1.84	1.93	0.08	22
NY	7.11	2.04	-5.07	5.11	2.00	-3.10	3
PA	1.86	2.57	0.71	2.04	2.44	0.40	26
IL	3.81	1.83	-1.97	2.71	1.80	-0.91	6
IN	4.26	1.99	-2.27	2.63	1.98	-0.65	12
IA	2.64	2.03	-0.62	2.72	1.97	-0.75	10
MO	1.70	2.56	0.86	2.19	2.53	0.34	25
OH	4.47	2.49	-1.98	2.46	2.48	0.02	21
MI	2.51	2.74	0.23	2.87	2.61	-0.26	17
MN	3.68	2.61	-1.07	3.08	2.55	-0.53	13
WI	3.55	2.42	-1.13	3.19	2.31	-0.88	8
KS	1.86	2.00	0.13	2.27	2.04	-0.23	19
NE	2.06	2.27	0.21	2.61	2.25	-0.36	14
ND	1.59	1.60	0.01	1.35	1.66	0.30	24
SD	0.86	2.40	1.54	1.07	2.42	1.35	39
KY	2.49	2.08	-0.41	1.63	2.13	0.50	29
NC	1.66	1.32	-0.34	3.49	1.29	-2.21	4
TN	1.10	2.74	1.64	1.72	2.75	1.03	37
VA	1.32	2.69	1.37	2.18	2.64	0.46	27
WV	1.34	2.62	1.28	0.69	2.62	1.93	48
AL	1.83	2.15	0.32	2.25	2.23	-0.03	20
FL	3.03	1.29	-1.74	4.56	1.28	-3.28	2
GA	1.06	2.02	0.95	2.88	2.00	-0.88	7
SC	1.62	1.95	0.33	1.54	2.02	0.48	28
AR	1.37	1.57	0.21	1.92	1.68	-0.24	18
LA	1.53	1.91	0.38	2.80	1.95	-0.85	9
MS	1.67	1.80	0.13	2.21	1.90	-0.31	15
OK	1.72	2.14	0.42	1.65	2.23	0.58	32
TX	4.37	1.91	-2.46	4.00	2.07	-1.93	5
AZ	1.28	1.77	0.49	1.64	1.90	0.26	23
CO	1.48	2.19	0.71	1.69	2.24	0.56	31
ID	0.85	2.13	1.28	1.19	2.14	0.95	35
MT	1.46	1.79	0.33	1.28	1.88	0.60	33
NV	0.55	2.03	1.48	0.46	2.09	1.63	44

Tab. A2.14 cont'd: *States' Contribution to the National Research Stock Compared to their Reception of Spillins, 1949, 1985.*

State	1949			1985			
	Research	Spillins	Net Gain	Research	Spillins	Net Gain	Rank
NM	0.72	2.14	1.42	0.64	2.25	1.61	43
UT	1.00	2.50	1.51	0.85	2.50	1.65	45
WY	0.96	1.92	0.96	0.58	2.01	1.43	41
CA	6.87	2.21	-4.66	9.62	2.13	-7.49	1
OR	2.14	2.40	0.26	2.67	2.39	-0.28	16
WA	1.81	2.07	0.26	2.75	2.02	-0.73	11

Table A2.15: *Extension Intensity Ratios by State, Five Year Intervals, Average Annual Growth Rate 1949-85, and Rank.*

State	1949	1955	1960	1965	1970	1975	1980	1985	Growth	Rank
CT	0.32	0.45	0.60	0.81	1.14	1.27	1.26	1.44	3.96	11
ME	0.21	0.29	0.44	0.49	0.76	0.65	0.80	1.45	4.91	10
MA	0.52	0.84	1.07	1.53	2.23	2.40	2.09	2.78	4.46	4
NH	0.53	0.70	1.00	1.54	2.09	2.22	2.57	3.16	4.80	2
RI	0.64	1.00	1.23	1.96	3.68	4.45	4.82	3.36	4.64	1
VT	0.23	0.40	0.47	0.61	0.82	0.82	0.70	0.96	3.80	22
DE	0.13	0.25	0.31	0.40	0.50	0.54	0.56	0.49	3.27	39
MD	0.33	0.55	0.71	0.87	1.02	0.89	0.97	1.06	3.10	20
NJ	0.32	0.54	0.69	1.12	1.57	2.42	2.33	2.44	5.60	5
NY	0.36	0.56	0.69	0.87	1.15	1.10	0.96	1.35	3.35	12
PA	0.20	0.31	0.40	0.50	0.62	0.61	0.53	0.63	2.82	33
IL	0.11	0.16	0.18	0.20	0.31	0.22	0.24	0.33	2.94	45
IN	0.15	0.22	0.29	0.32	0.41	0.30	0.33	0.52	3.41	37
IA	0.09	0.11	0.16	0.17	0.19	0.16	0.15	0.25	2.84	48
MO	0.17	0.21	0.30	0.37	0.51	0.46	0.42	0.56	3.58	36
OH	0.15	0.22	0.32	0.39	0.57	0.46	0.45	0.63	3.92	31
MI	0.24	0.47	0.62	0.73	0.95	0.84	0.81	0.75	2.96	26
MN	0.09	0.13	0.17	0.21	0.28	0.24	0.25	0.35	3.48	44
WI	0.13	0.20	0.28	0.34	0.40	0.35	0.34	0.50	3.55	38
KS	0.19	0.33	0.29	0.44	0.43	0.36	0.34	0.47	2.45	40
NE	0.10	0.16	0.16	0.23	0.25	0.20	0.20	0.27	2.89	46
ND	0.12	0.14	0.21	0.22	0.33	0.18	0.31	0.39	3.28	42
SD	0.10	0.16	0.19	0.22	0.24	0.23	0.21	0.25	2.29	47
KY	0.25	0.39	0.50	0.58	0.74	0.72	0.72	1.07	3.75	19
NC	0.35	0.47	0.59	0.76	0.91	0.79	0.83	1.10	2.95	18
TN	0.30	0.44	0.57	0.76	0.96	0.94	0.93	1.13	3.40	16
VA	0.36	0.56	0.72	0.97	1.38	1.52	1.44	1.84	4.36	8
WV	0.53	0.77	1.16	1.76	2.33	2.42	2.30	3.08	4.57	3
AL	0.46	0.52	0.66	0.80	1.03	0.89	0.99	1.13	2.11	17
FL	0.24	0.30	0.35	0.44	0.68	0.55	0.53	0.72	2.82	28
GA	0.38	0.41	0.59	0.70	0.89	0.79	0.99	1.22	3.08	14
SC	0.42	0.52	0.69	0.82	1.14	1.12	1.51	1.86	3.89	7
AR	0.27	0.31	0.47	0.47	0.53	0.46	0.49	0.57	1.82	35
LA	0.51	0.68	1.01	1.11	1.09	1.09	1.00	1.95	3.30	6
MS	0.42	0.45	0.65	0.63	0.76	0.88	0.89	1.30	3.10	13

Tab. A2.15 cont'd: *Extension Intensity Ratios by State, Five Year Intervals, Average Annual Growth Rate 1949-85, and Rank.*

State	1949	1955	1960	1965	1970	1975	1980	1985	Growth	Rank
OK	0.24	0.47	0.51	0.56	0.58	0.52	0.46	0.83	2.98	25
TX	0.15	0.27	0.32	0.36	0.47	0.45	0.47	0.73	3.90	27
AZ	0.18	0.18	0.27	0.35	0.45	0.43	0.38	0.60	3.40	34
CO	0.14	0.32	0.28	0.40	0.38	0.36	0.42	0.64	3.79	30
ID	0.18	0.24	0.32	0.34	0.35	0.29	0.27	0.36	1.63	43
MT	0.18	0.20	0.31	0.30	0.34	0.27	0.31	0.70	3.41	29
NV	0.40	0.57	0.84	1.16	1.26	1.28	1.11	1.75	3.94	9
NM	0.34	0.53	0.62	0.80	0.75	0.64	0.55	0.87	2.31	24
UT	0.27	0.37	0.52	0.73	0.69	0.70	0.78	1.14	3.99	15
WY	0.33	0.46	0.49	0.58	0.59	0.50	0.50	1.03	3.27	21
CA	0.16	0.21	0.26	0.30	0.38	0.29	0.30	0.41	2.45	41
OR	0.34	0.57	0.74	0.85	0.99	0.73	0.67	0.92	2.35	23
WA	0.23	0.30	0.43	0.54	0.61	0.37	0.45	0.63	2.43	32

Table A2.16: *Level and Growth Rates of Total Factor Productivity Levels (1949=1.00), Calculated Using Explicit Output Quantity Index.*

State	1955	1960	1965	1970	1975	1980	1985	Growth
CT	1.19	1.13	1.29	1.29	1.35	1.24	1.38	0.73
ME	1.19	1.21	1.35	1.49	1.50	1.42	1.54	1.08
MA	1.29	1.24	1.43	1.45	1.51	1.48	1.38	0.76
NH	1.45	1.40	1.62	1.55	1.58	1.50	1.49	0.84
RI	1.30	1.28	1.54	1.73	1.84	1.75	2.54	2.20
VT	1.11	1.10	1.17	1.17	1.14	1.08	1.09	0.22
DE	1.05	1.16	1.24	1.31	1.48	1.27	1.56	1.06
MD	1.02	1.09	1.15	1.19	1.29	1.14	1.41	0.89
NJ	1.15	1.32	1.40	1.20	1.02	0.96	1.28	0.31
NY	1.09	1.08	1.16	1.20	1.20	1.24	1.32	0.64
PA	1.02	1.05	1.13	1.18	1.20	1.18	1.40	0.84
IL	0.99	1.02	1.10	0.97	1.20	1.10	1.35	0.67
IN	0.99	1.03	1.08	1.03	1.14	1.15	1.32	0.68
IA	0.96	1.01	1.02	1.01	1.03	1.15	1.22	0.43
MO	0.99	1.03	1.05	1.05	1.11	1.08	1.30	0.55
OH	1.01	1.02	1.03	1.02	1.15	1.19	1.39	0.83
MI	0.95	0.97	1.05	1.11	1.19	1.24	1.41	0.87
MN	1.02	1.02	1.02	1.10	1.11	1.20	1.33	0.74
WI	1.04	1.03	1.08	1.11	1.10	1.13	1.18	0.43
KS	0.92	1.19	1.12	1.18	1.27	1.20	1.40	0.77
NE	0.96	1.08	1.05	1.12	1.19	1.19	1.46	0.83
ND	1.12	1.11	1.33	1.21	1.40	1.03	1.72	1.29
SD	1.04	1.14	1.18	1.24	1.11	1.23	1.48	1.01
KY	0.99	1.06	1.16	1.18	1.31	1.22	1.36	0.96
NC	1.09	1.18	1.23	1.38	1.52	1.42	1.50	1.12
TN	1.05	1.10	1.18	1.18	1.34	1.32	1.57	1.30
VA	0.99	1.08	1.10	1.16	1.24	1.12	1.30	0.73
WV	1.17	1.29	1.27	1.41	1.46	1.37	1.44	1.01
AL	1.19	1.26	1.39	1.39	1.65	1.50	1.75	1.69
FL	1.03	0.94	1.02	1.01	1.20	1.12	1.10	0.25
GA	1.12	1.21	1.32	1.38	1.59	1.42	1.72	1.52
SC	1.23	1.31	1.51	1.58	1.82	1.60	1.81	1.73
AR	1.09	1.14	1.22	1.27	1.50	1.38	1.61	1.38
LA	1.06	1.07	1.18	1.32	1.39	1.33	1.46	1.24
MS	1.26	1.36	1.61	1.73	1.75	1.69	1.98	1.87
OK	0.92	1.13	1.10	1.11	1.25	1.17	1.28	0.83
TX	0.88	0.98	0.97	0.97	1.17	1.03	1.22	0.69
AZ	0.98	0.94	0.96	0.92	0.98	1.04	1.09	0.30
CO	0.89	1.02	0.93	1.08	1.19	1.10	1.20	0.49
ID	1.03	1.01	1.10	1.16	1.19	1.22	1.28	0.67
MT	1.19	1.04	1.16	1.18	1.32	1.17	0.90	-0.03
NV	1.08	1.05	1.08	1.13	1.15	1.11	1.20	0.63
NM	0.95	1.03	0.93	1.08	1.11	1.09	1.34	0.83

Tab. A2.16 cont'd: *Levels and Growth Rates of Total Factor Productivity (1949=1.00) Calculated Using the Explicit Output Quantity Index.*

State	1955	1960	1965	1970	1975	1980	1985	Growth
UT	1.17	1.12	1.16	1.28	1.28	1.20	1.29	0.64
WY	1.06	1.09	1.14	0.85	0.95	0.93	0.91	-0.30
CA	1.02	0.98	1.01	1.03	1.19	1.15	1.22	0.54
OR	1.01	1.04	1.07	1.12	1.20	1.21	1.29	0.73
WA	0.99	0.97	1.03	1.09	1.02	1.08	1.13	0.42

Table A2.17: *Levels and Growth Rates of Total Factor Productivity (1949=1.00) Calculated Using Implicit Output Quantity Index*

State	1955	1960	1965	1970	1975	1980	1985	Growth
CT	1.17	1.28	1.42	1.44	1.47	1.34	1.43	0.76
ME	1.13	1.13	1.19	1.35	1.35	1.13	1.30	0.64
MA	1.28	1.42	1.59	1.60	1.64	1.65	1.22	0.64
NH	1.45	1.39	1.59	1.53	1.55	1.36	1.40	0.72
RI	1.32	1.47	1.72	1.85	1.87	1.80	2.36	2.03
VT	1.13	1.15	1.14	1.20	1.13	1.12	1.10	0.20
DE	1.05	1.17	1.25	1.29	1.46	1.25	1.57	1.04
MD	0.99	1.09	1.13	1.18	1.24	1.09	1.33	0.78
NJ	1.06	1.44	1.55	1.20	1.18	1.11	1.40	0.61
NY	1.09	1.15	1.20	1.23	1.24	1.30	1.35	0.68
PA	1.00	1.10	1.16	1.21	1.22	1.18	1.38	0.88
IL	1.05	1.06	1.22	0.99	1.43	0.98	1.43	0.93
IN	1.01	1.07	1.17	1.04	1.22	1.03	1.27	0.77
IA	0.98	1.04	1.14	1.08	1.14	1.15	1.33	0.63
MO	1.05	1.03	1.13	1.10	1.09	0.93	1.33	0.53
OH	1.01	1.07	1.10	1.08	1.21	1.10	1.39	0.95
MI	0.93	0.96	1.05	1.14	1.19	1.18	1.41	0.98
MN	1.04	1.07	1.09	1.16	1.13	1.15	1.35	0.90
WI	1.01	1.01	1.07	1.10	1.06	1.12	1.10	0.36
KS	0.92	1.25	1.30	1.31	1.31	1.13	1.50	0.87
NE	0.92	1.14	1.20	1.19	1.25	1.12	1.56	0.95
ND	1.31	1.36	1.70	1.46	1.69	0.88	2.21	1.85
SD	1.12	1.45	1.45	1.49	1.25	1.31	1.66	1.26
KY	0.97	1.06	1.16	1.12	1.25	1.02	1.15	0.82
NC	1.08	1.14	1.18	1.32	1.42	1.31	1.38	0.91
TN	1.06	1.07	1.12	1.15	1.23	1.14	1.35	0.97
VA	0.98	1.06	1.06	1.09	1.15	0.99	1.15	0.44
WV	1.12	1.26	1.17	1.30	1.35	1.31	1.20	0.69
AL	1.19	1.20	1.30	1.33	1.52	1.35	1.58	1.40
FL	1.03	0.96	1.06	1.05	1.24	1.18	1.12	0.28
GA	1.09	1.15	1.25	1.29	1.44	1.26	1.55	1.25
SC	1.18	1.24	1.45	1.53	1.69	1.35	1.69	1.54
AR	1.14	1.14	1.20	1.32	1.52	1.30	1.62	1.42
LA	1.06	1.07	1.13	1.30	1.31	1.18	1.33	1.01
MS	1.42	1.41	1.63	1.94	1.80	1.57	1.97	1.84
OK	0.91	1.13	1.13	1.14	1.19	1.05	1.27	0.86
TX	0.84	0.95	0.99	1.05	1.08	0.90	1.20	0.75
AZ	0.97	0.95	0.98	0.98	0.96	1.13	1.18	0.58
CO	0.91	1.06	1.06	1.19	1.22	1.12	1.23	0.55
ID	1.02	1.00	1.16	1.20	1.16	1.20	1.25	0.59
MT	1.48	1.24	1.54	1.61	1.68	1.45	0.99	0.08
NV	1.04	0.99	1.01	1.09	1.13	1.16	1.16	0.51
NM	1.01	1.06	1.01	1.16	1.07	0.95	1.34	0.91

Tab. A2.17 cont'd: *Levels and Growth Rates of Total Factor Productivity (1949=1.00) Calculated Using Implicit Output Quantity Index.*

State	1955	1960	1965	1970	1975	1980	1985	Growth
UT	1.14	1.09	1.20	1.28	1.23	1.19	1.25	0.54
WY	1.14	1.06	1.19	1.24	1.17	1.11	0.99	-0.07
CA	1.03	1.03	1.05	1.09	1.25	1.21	1.28	0.68
OR	1.01	1.08	1.12	1.18	1.24	1.29	1.34	0.79
WA	1.00	0.99	1.08	1.16	1.08	1.08	1.12	0.42

Table A3.1:   *Partial Factor Productivity for Land by State, 1949-85.*

State	Productivity Level 1949	Productivity Level 1985	Avg. growth	Dev. from avg. 1949	Deviat from avg. 1985	Convergence
CT	20.19	49.53	2.52	1282.8	595.63	Yes
ME	9.28	27.22	3.03	535.7	282.35	Yes
MA	18.49	36.60	1.91	1166.4	414.09	Yes
NH	8.32	20.41	2.52	469.6	186.61	Yes
RI	14.18	76.35	4.79	870.7	972.42	No
VT	7.80	18.06	2.36	434.1	153.68	Yes
DE	5.45	18.57	3.47	272.9	160.79	Yes
MD	4.85	15.97	3.36	232.4	124.33	Yes
NJ	14.34	26.00	1.67	882.1	265.23	Yes
NY	6.35	14.93	2.41	334.6	109.77	Yes
PA	5.72	16.52	2.99	291.4	132.02	Yes
IL	1.65	3.85	2.39	12.9	-45.87	No
IN	1.72	4.19	2.51	17.6	-41.10	No
IA	1.68	3.92	2.38	15.2	-44.91	No
MO	1.93	3.49	1.65	32.5	-51.03	No
OH	2.07	5.12	2.55	41.6	-28.10	Yes
MI	3.03	7.55	2.57	107.2	6.07	Yes
MN	2.06	5.48	2.75	41.3	-23.00	Yes
WI	4.12	8.30	1.96	182.4	16.60	Yes
KS	2.27	6.35	2.90	55.4	-10.83	Yes
NE	1.79	5.75	3.29	22.7	-19.19	Yes
ND	1.29	4.61	3.61	-11.8	-35.19	No
SD	1.62	4.94	3.15	10.7	-30.60	No
KY	2.58	5.84	2.29	76.6	-18.04	Yes
NC	6.61	15.90	2.47	352.5	123.32	Yes
TN	2.55	5.97	2.39	74.7	-16.15	Yes
VA	4.53	8.95	1.91	210.1	25.72	Yes
WV	3.83	6.29	1.39	162.4	-11.65	Yes
AL	2.85	11.72	4.00	95.2	64.55	Yes
FL	5.41	16.01	3.06	270.3	124.91	Yes
GA	2.67	12.67	4.42	82.6	77.94	Yes
SC	5.45	13.22	2.49	273.1	85.70	Yes
AR	2.77	8.23	3.08	89.4	15.66	Yes
LA	3.12	6.28	1.96	113.9	-11.72	Yes
MS	3.04	8.15	2.77	108.2	14.42	Yes
OK	3.13	5.93	1.79	114.2	-16.76	Yes
TX	4.15	7.44	1.63	184.5	4.53	Yes
AZ	0.96	2.76	2.98	-34.3	-61.19	No
CO	2.81	7.78	2.87	92.3	9.31	Yes
ID	1.04	2.47	2.44	-29.0	-65.37	No
MT	1.00	1.62	1.35	-31.5	-77.24	No
NV	0.26	0.52	1.97	-82.4	-92.69	No
NM	1.76	4.02	2.32	20.4	-43.53	No

Tab. A3.1 cont'd: *Changes in Partial Factor Productivity for Land by State, 1949-85.*

State	Productivity Level 1949	Productivity Level 1985	Avg. growth	Dev. from avg. 1949	Deviat from avg. 1985	Convergence
UT	0.55	1.09	1.91	-62.2	-84.67	No
WY	1.34	2.25	1.46	-8.5	-68.36	No
CA	3.20	9.09	2.94	118.9	27.62	Yes
OR	0.83	2.05	2.55	-43.4	-71.27	No
WA	1.95	4.40	2.29	33.4	-38.22	No

Table A3.2: *Partial Factor Productivity for Labor by State, 1949-85.*

State	Productivity Level 1949	Productivity Level 1985	Avg. growth	Dev. from avg. 1949	Deviat from avg. 1985	Convergence
CT	1.64	7.28	4.22	12.46	2.22	Yes
ME	1.29	6.42	4.56	-11.66	-9.79	Yes
MA	1.27	4.18	3.37	-13.18	-41.31	No
NH	0.89	2.79	3.22	-39.14	-60.86	No
RI	1.35	9.23	5.49	-7.70	29.64	No
VT	1.15	4.63	3.95	-21.52	-34.96	No
DE	1.72	13.95	5.98	18.11	95.96	No
MD	1.39	7.33	4.73	-4.92	2.99	Yes
NJ	2.05	5.97	3.01	40.46	-16.18	Yes
NY	1.33	5.05	3.77	-8.65	-29.02	No
PA	1.18	5.38	4.30	-19.05	-24.50	No
IL	1.76	8.93	4.61	20.77	25.47	No
IN	1.30	6.70	4.65	-10.65	-5.86	Yes
IA	1.72	7.85	4.30	17.91	10.28	Yes
MO	1.02	4.23	4.04	-30.31	-40.53	No
OH	1.10	5.51	4.57	-24.40	-22.57	Yes
MI	0.99	5.22	4.73	-32.27	-26.71	Yes
MN	1.27	6.10	4.47	-13.36	-14.35	No
WI	1.40	4.58	3.34	-4.01	-35.70	No
KS	1.45	8.84	5.16	-0.98	24.17	No
NE	1.58	10.53	5.41	8.17	47.96	No
ND	1.40	8.27	5.06	-4.28	16.19	No
SD	1.34	6.75	4.58	-8.01	-5.26	Yes
KY	0.78	3.54	4.28	-46.46	-50.27	No
NC	0.64	4.93	5.81	-55.85	-30.73	Yes
TN	0.58	3.03	4.72	-60.61	-57.45	Yes
VA	0.81	3.58	4.22	-44.54	-49.68	No
WV	0.47	1.45	3.17	-67.61	-79.60	No
AL	0.45	5.11	6.98	-69.18	-28.26	Yes
FL	1.66	10.45	5.25	13.34	46.85	No
GA	0.51	7.22	7.67	-65.42	1.38	Yes
SC	0.56	4.35	5.86	-61.63	-38.87	Yes
AR	0.65	7.57	7.04	-55.20	6.37	Yes
LA	0.85	6.55	5.84	-41.82	-7.99	Yes
MS	0.43	6.39	7.75	-70.22	-10.21	Yes
OK	1.10	5.28	4.47	-24.97	-25.80	No
TX	1.57	7.25	4.34	7.56	1.89	Yes
AZ	5.15	24.22	4.39	252.83	240.12	Yes
CO	2.41	11.85	4.52	65.22	66.48	No
ID	1.87	8.86	4.41	28.31	24.43	Yes
MT	1.54	3.91	2.63	5.31	-45.03	No
NV	4.03	8.83	2.20	176.27	24.05	Yes
NM	2.05	9.74	4.43	40.14	36.80	Yes

Tab. A3.2 cont.: *Partial Factor Productivity for Labor by State, 1949-85.*

State	Productivity Level 1949	Productivity Level 1985	Avg. annual growth	Deviat from avg. 1949	Deviat from avg. 1985	Convergence
UT	1.49	4.70	3.25	1.86	-33.94	No
WY	2.42	6.19	2.64	65.97	-13.09	Yes
CA	3.67	18.47	4.59	151.48	159.38	No
OR	1.37	5.54	3.95	-6.07	-22.16	No
WA	1.42	6.98	4.52	-2.50	-1.92	Yes

Table A3.3:   *Changes in Partial Factor Productivity for Purchased Inputs by State, 1949-85.*

State	Productivity Level 1949	Productivity Level 1985	Avg. growth	Dev. from avg. 1949	Deviat from avg. 1985	Convergence
CT	1.93	2.29	0.47	32.48	-67.83	No
ME	2.40	2.38	-0.02	64.58	-66.52	No
MA	1.77	2.01	0.36	21.10	-71.74	No
NH	1.47	1.61	0.27	0.36	-77.35	No
RI	1.46	3.95	2.80	0.27	-44.46	No
VT	1.98	1.82	-0.24	35.85	-74.44	No
DE	1.17	1.78	1.17	-20.06	-75.07	No
MD	1.83	2.00	0.25	25.09	-71.95	No
NJ	1.66	2.77	1.43	13.78	-61.13	No
NY	1.95	2.12	0.24	33.26	-70.18	No
PA	1.97	2.24	0.36	34.80	-68.48	No
IL	3.43	3.23	-0.16	134.67	-54.59	Yes
IN	2.87	2.70	-0.17	96.31	-62.06	Yes
IA	3.16	2.81	-0.33	116.25	-60.57	Yes
MO	3.24	2.56	-0.65	121.76	-64.05	Yes
OH	2.46	2.78	0.33	68.58	-61.01	Yes
MI	2.62	2.45	-0.19	79.50	-65.63	Yes
MN	2.71	2.56	-0.16	85.30	-64.08	Yes
WI	2.96	2.21	-0.81	102.85	-68.94	Yes
KS	3.20	2.83	-0.34	119.01	-60.25	Yes
NE	3.05	3.31	0.22	109.08	-53.52	Yes
ND	2.65	3.98	1.14	81.20	-44.04	Yes
SD	2.54	3.20	0.65	73.70	-55.02	Yes
KY	4.34	3.11	-0.92	197.01	-56.37	Yes
NC	3.44	1.99	-1.51	135.35	-72.05	Yes
TN	3.60	2.51	-0.99	146.40	-64.72	Yes
VA	2.71	1.94	-0.92	85.65	-72.70	Yes
WV	2.33	1.50	-1.23	59.72	-78.98	No
AL	2.74	2.03	-0.83	87.43	-71.52	Yes
FL	3.20	2.84	-0.33	119.05	-60.13	Yes
GA	2.16	2.08	-0.10	47.77	-70.80	No
SC	2.93	2.15	-0.85	100.56	-69.74	Yes
AR	3.00	2.76	-0.23	105.69	-61.17	Yes
LA	3.85	2.82	-0.86	163.48	-60.38	Yes
MS	3.10	2.76	-0.32	112.60	-61.18	Yes
OK	3.36	2.79	-0.52	130.01	-60.83	Yes
TX	3.42	2.77	-0.58	133.95	-61.15	Yes
AZ	3.22	2.51	-0.69	120.38	-64.79	Yes
CO	3.31	2.94	-0.33	126.97	-58.71	Yes
ID	3.02	2.56	-0.46	106.63	-64.03	Yes
MT	2.29	1.89	-0.53	57.01	-73.41	No
NV	3.22	1.73	-1.71	120.38	-75.74	Yes

Table A3.3 cont'd: *Changes in Partial Factor Productivity for Purchased Inputs by State, 1949-85.*

State	Productivity Level 1949	Productivity Level 1985	Avg. annual growth	Deviat from avg. 1949	Deviat from avg. 1985	Convergence
NM	3.73	2.73	-0.86	155.46	-61.60	Yes
UT	2.43	1.80	-0.83	66.25	-74.75	No
WY	2.94	2.47	-0.48	101.00	-65.36	Yes
CA	2.65	2.77	0.12	81.59	-61.10	Yes
OR	2.45	2.48	0.04	67.66	-65.15	Yes
WA	2.57	2.28	-0.33	76.04	-67.98	Yes

Table A3.4: *Coefficients of the Production Function with Human Capital.*

Coefficient	Parameter Estimate	Standard Error	t-statistic
Intercept	-22.8877	0.1759	-130.1140
Labor	0.2627	0.0064	41.1990
Hum. Cap.	0.0762	0.0012	61.2840
P.Input	0.3430	0.0021	164.0880
Capital	0.3181	0.0058	54.7300
Time x Time	0.1437	0.0028	50.8190
Time^2	-0.0010	0.0000	-32.9170
Labor x Labor	-0.0081	0.0010	-7.8250
Labor x Hum. Cap.	0.0120	0.0007	16.1740
Labor x P.Input	0.0527	0.0010	53.2580
Labor x Capital	-0.0566	0.0008	-71.1200
Labor x Time	-0.0180	0.0002	-72.8110
Hum. C x Hum. Cap.	0.0115	0.0008	13.8930
Hum. Cap. x P.Input	0.0006	0.0008	0.8510
Hum. Cap. x Capital	-0.0242	0.0005	-46.3700
Hum. Cap. x Time	0.0027	0.0001	46.0470
P.Input x P.Input	0.0472	0.0010	46.6920
P.Input x Capital	-0.1005	0.0008	-133.6170
P.Input x Time	0.0053	0.0001	48.0730
Capital x Capital	0.1813	0.0007	272.5690
Capital x Time	-0.0014	0.0001	-19.4610

Table A3.5: *Simple Correlation Between Variables Used in the Cost- and Production Functions.*

	HC	Labor	LD	PI	FC	R	E	S	OTP	CST	P_{LB}	P_{LD}	P_{PC}	P_{FC}
HC	1.00	0.84	0.76	0.92	0.95	0.67	0.84	0.17	0.92	0.93	0.06	0.08	0.02	-0.05
LB	0.84	1.00	0.68	0.71	0.76	0.34	0.68	-0.28	0.74	0.83	-0.38	-0.23	-0.28	-0.38
LD	0.76	0.68	1.00	0.79	0.82	0.44	0.56	0.05	0.84	0.92	-0.04	-0.22	-0.06	-0.19
PC	0.92	0.71	0.79	1.00	0.94	0.79	0.85	0.25	0.98	0.94	0.21	0.16	0.16	0.10
FC	0.95	0.76	0.82	0.94	1.00	0.74	0.86	0.30	0.94	0.95	0.22	0.19	0.21	0.10
R	0.67	0.34	0.44	0.79	0.74	1.00	0.83	0.54	0.75	0.64	0.55	0.50	0.46	0.46
E	0.84	0.68	0.56	0.85	0.86	0.83	1.00	0.34	0.82	0.79	0.28	0.33	0.26	0.22
S	0.17	-0.28	0.05	0.25	0.30	0.54	0.34	1.00	0.19	0.11	0.91	0.75	0.75	0.78
OP	0.92	0.74	0.84	0.98	0.94	0.75	0.82	0.19	1.00	0.96	0.16	0.10	0.12	0.05
CS	0.93	0.83	0.92	0.94	0.95	0.64	0.79	0.11	0.96	1.00	0.03	-0.03	0.02	-0.08
P_{LB}	0.06	-0.38	-0.04	0.21	0.22	0.55	0.28	0.91	0.16	0.03	1.00	0.85	0.89	0.90
P_{LD}	0.08	-0.23	-0.22	0.16	0.19	0.50	0.33	0.75	0.10	-0.03	0.85	1.00	0.85	0.86
P_{PC}	0.02	-0.28	-0.06	0.16	0.21	0.46	0.26	0.75	0.12	0.02	0.89	0.85	1.00	0.94
P_{FC}	-0.05	-0.38	-0.19	0.10	0.10	0.46	0.22	0.78	0.05	-0.08	0.90	0.86	0.94	1.00

Note: HC = Human Capital, LB = Labor, LD = Land, PI = Purchased Inputs, FC = Capital, R = Research, E = Extension, S = Spillovers, OTP = Output, CST = Total Cost, P_{LB} = Price of Labor, P_{LD} = Price of Land, P_{PC} = Price of purchased inputs, P_{FC} = Price of Capital

Table A 3.6: Average Correlation of Output Between Varioius States, 1949-80.

	NJ	PA	IA	MN	NE	NC	FL	AR	TX	CO	CA
CT	80.9	81.1	17.4	45.9	17.9	51.4	39.1	24.5	25.0	25.3	64.4
DE	20.9	26.0	22.0	25.4	17.7	30.1	12.6	50.5	13.6	9.7	18.5
ME	53.0	59.3	12.3	33.8	13.8	22.4	26.0	28.4	19.6	22.9	48.4
MA	89.9	86.2	21.1	51.1	20.0	34.1	41.3	21.4	25.9	27.0	69.2
NH	82.9	92.0	21.3	55.4	23.3	24.1	35.0	23.9	29.4	31.7	70.1
NJ	100.0	77.7	30.3	53.8	27.7	25.6	39.8	24.6	25.8	27.8	65.5
RI	84.7	75.3	17.3	43.3	16.2	21.2	41.1	19.0	22.3	24.0	63.4
MD	57.3	77.0	47.5	67.6	45.6	51.7	32.6	49.2	33.6	36.7	55.5
NY	70.8	95.6	26.2	63.2	28.4	22.7	34.6	19.8	30.3	35.2	70.7
PA	77.7	100.0	42.7	74.9	44.5	32.1	37.8	26.8	37.3	43.9	73.0
VT	62.3	91.6	20.0	57.5	22.2	19.8	30.9	17.9	27.2	31.5	66.1
IL	30.6	40.9	94.7	85.9	77.8	33.1	17.7	33.7	27.4	37.9	23.6
IN	37.5	48.5	96.1	89.0	78.3	36.9	20.8	34.5	29.7	40.0	29.6
IA	30.3	42.7	100.0	88.0	85.0	33.9	21.3	31.8	38.2	49.2	30.1
MO	40.0	54.6	88.8	89.1	85.9	34.3	29.6	51.7	61.7	70.1	51.8
OH	57.3	72.0	87.5	96.3	77.1	39.1	30.6	39.7	38.8	50.9	50.6
MI	69.3	91.6	65.7	90.0	67.1	33.1	36.7	29.4	43.3	56.6	68.5
MN	53.8	74.9	88.0	100.0	80.9	36.2	31.2	37.7	45.8	58.9	55.8
WI	64.6	95.6	47.3	78.2	46.2	28.0	34.7	22.6	36.7	43.2	68.4

Tab. A.3.6 cont'd: *Average Correlation of Output Between Various States, 1949-80.*

	NJ	PA	IA	MN	NE	NC	FL	AR	TX	CO	CA
KA	24.0	37.1	48.5	56.6	78.7	17.5	23.3	28.8	66.4	86.4	44.2
NE	27.7	44.5	85.0	80.9	100.0	27.4	25.7	29.3	63.3	82.2	43.4
ND	20.4	31.9	28.2	44.2	54.8	11.8	16.2	20.5	44.1	69.0	37.5
SD	29.9	47.9	75.0	77.6	92.7	24.4	28.9	32.2	69.2	90.0	51.8
KY	36.2	52.4	57.3	64.1	59.4	86.1	29.2	27.4	41.4	50.9	42.6
NC	25.6	32.1	33.9	36.2	27.4	100.0	20.3	29.9	19.6	16.5	23.6
TN	52.2	66.6	67.7	79.2	67.6	62.0	36.6	61.7	69.6	61.3	68.0
VA	58.5	78.0	57.7	76.1	62.5	72.3	38.5	41.3	51.0	60.2	64.6
WV	60.7	81.0	47.8	70.7	61.4	33.0	35.5	38.2	56.6	69.8	72.4
AL	39.4	47.3	51.7	56.3	53.5	39.5	29.7	80.7	70.0	48.6	59.0
FL	39.8	37.8	21.3	31.2	25.7	20.3	100.0	18.0	28.1	29.9	49.6
GA	41.5	48.2	51.5	54.5	46.4	61.7	28.0	65.4	49.2	33.7	47.5
SC	38.4	42.2	49.2	54.6	41.6	83.6	25.3	61.3	49.5	30.8	46.5
AR	24.6	26.8	31.8	37.7	29.3	29.9	18.0	100.0	62.4	29.6	49.2
LA	33.4	40.1	40.2	50.5	42.2	23.0	29.1	78.6	67.5	44.2	59.9
MS	28.6	33.0	37.8	44.3	37.6	28.9	21.1	89.7	73.5	36.9	58.3
OK	26.7	41.0	41.0	52.9	74.1	16.5	28.3	38.9	79.6	92.8	57.7
TX	25.8	37.3	38.2	45.8	63.3	19.6	28.1	62.4	100.0	74.0	67.3

Tab.A 3.6 cont'd: *Average Correlation of Output Between Various States, 1949-80.*

	NJ	PA	IA	MN	NE	NC	FL	AR	TX	CO	CA
AZ	22.5	33.8	26.2	36.4	45.2	15.0	26.0	57.1	88.2	58.6	71.7
CO	27.8	43.9	49.2	58.9	82.2	16.5	29.9	29.6	74.0	100.0	57.9
ID	37.4	55.7	31.7	53.7	58.1	15.1	27.9	24.2	53.8	80.1	60.5
MT	18.4	31.8	32.4	44.6	67.3	10.9	20.8	24.8	61.1	88.0	46.0
NV	26.2	44.6	38.8	51.1	67.9	12.0	27.3	28.3	67.4	88.4	58.5
NM	25.5	40.9	39.8	49.5	68.9	16.1	29.4	49.2	92.3	86.4	67.3
UT	51.9	73.7	39.0	65.4	62.0	20.2	33.5	30.0	61.5	82.1	74.4
WY	19.9	35.7	40.5	48.7	72.7	11.4	26.0	27.9	70.6	94.2	53.9
CA	65.5	73.0	30.1	55.8	43.4	23.6	49.6	49.2	67.3	57.9	100.0
OR	50.9	63.9	37.4	60.9	64.5	19.4	34.6	30.8	62.2	85.7	70.4
WA	48.1	61.4	25.3	51.7	48.1	17.7	26.4	23.4	43.9	64.6	57.8

REFERENCES

Adams, J.D. 1990, Fundamental Stocks of Knowledge and Productivity Growth, Journal of Political Economy 98 (1990), 673-702

Adusei, E.O., Norton, G.W. 1990, The Magnitude of Agricultural Maintenance Research in the USA, Journal of Production Agriculture 3 (1990), 1-6

Alston, J.M., Edwards, G.W., Freebairn, J.W. 1988, Market Distortions and Benefits from Research, American Journal of Agricultural Economics 70 (1988), 281-288

Alston, J.M., Pardey, P.G. 1993, Market Distortions and Technological Progress in Agriculture, Technological Forecasting and Social Change 43 (1993), 301-319

Aly, H.Y., Grabowski, R. 1989, Measuring the Rate and Bias of Technical Innovation in Japanese Agriculture: An alternative approach, European Review of Agricultural Economics 16 (1998), 65-81

Antle, J.M. 1984, The Structure of US Agricultural Technology: 1910-78, American Journal of Agricultural Economics 66 (1984), 414-421

Archibald, S.O., Brandt, L. 1991, A Flexible Model of Factor Biased Technological Change, Journal of Development Economics 35 (1992), 127-145

Arrow, K.J. 1962, The Economic Implications of Learning by Doing, Review of Economic Studies 39 (1962), 155-173

Azam, Q.T., Bloom, E.A., Evenson, R.E. 1991, Agricultural Research Productivity in Pakistan, Economic Growth Center Discussion Paper 644, Yale University, New Haven, CT

Backus, D., Kehoe, P, Kehoe, T. 1992, In Search of Scale Effects in Trade and Growth, Research Department Staff Report 152, Federal Reserve Bank of Minneapolis

Ball, V.E. 1985, Output, Input, and Productivity Measurement in US Agriculture, 1948-79, American Journal of Agricultural Economics (1985), 475-486

Barten, P. 1967, Maximum Likelihood Estimators of a Complete System of Consumer Demand Equations, European Economic Review 1 (1967), 7-73

Barro, R. 1991, Economic Growth in a Cross Section of Countries, Quarterly Journal of Economics 106 (1991), 407-443

Barro, R.J. 1990, Government Spending in a Simple Model of Endogenous Growth, Journal of Political Economy 98 (1990), S103-S125

Baumol, W.J. 1986, Productivity Growth, Convergence, and Welfare: What the Long-Run Data Show, American Economic Review 76 (1986), 1072-85

Baumol, W.J., Wolff, E.N. 1988, Productivity Growth, Convergence, and Welfare: Reply, American Economic Review 78 (1988), 1155-59

Benhabib, J., Jovanovich, B. 1990, Growth Accounting and Externalities, CV Starr Center, Paper

Bernstein, J.I. 1988, Costs of Production, Intra- and Interindustry R&D Spillovers: Canadian Evidence, Canadian Journal of Economics 21 (1988), 324-347

Bernstein, J.I. 1989, The Structure of Canadian Inter-industry R&D Spillovers, and the Rates of Return to R&D, Journal of Industrial Economics 37 (1989), 315-328

Bernstein, J.I., Nadiri, M.I. 1988, Interindustry R&D Spillovers, Rates of Return, and Production in High-Tech Industries, American Economic Review 78 (1988), 429-434

Bernstein, J.I., Nadiri, M.I. 1989, Research and Development and Intra-Industry Spillovers: An Empirical Application of Dynamic Duality, Review of Economic Studies 56 (1989), 249-269

Binswanger, H.P. 1974, The Measurement of Technical Change Biases with Many Factors of Production, American Economic Review 64 (1974), 964-976

Binswanger, H.P., Yang, M.C., Bowers, A., Mundlak, Y. 1987, On the Determinants of Cross-Country Aggregate Agricultural Supply, Journal of Econometrics 36 (1987), 111-131

Brown, R.S., Christensen, L.R. 1981, Estimating Elasticities of Substitution in a Model of Partial Static Equilibrium: An Application to US Agriculture 1947 to 1974, in: Berndt, E.R., Fields, B.C. (Eds), Modeling and Measuring Natural Resource Substitution, MIT Press

Capalbo, S.M., Antle, J.M. 1988, Agricultural Productivity Measurement and Explanation, Resources for the Future, Washington

Capalbo, S.M., Ball, V.E., Denny, M.G.S. 1991, International Comparisons of Agricultural Productivity: Development and Usefulness, American Journal of Agricultural Economics 72 (1991), 1292-1297

Capalbo, S.M., Vo, T.T. 1988, A Review of the Evidence on Agricultural Productivity and Aggregate Technology, Chapter 3 in Capalbo and Antle 1988

Chavas, J.P., Cox, T.L. 1992, A Nonparametric Analysis of the Influence of Research on Agricultural Productivity, American Journal of Agricultural Economics 74 (1992), 583-591

Costello, D.M. 1993, A Cross-Country, Cross-Industry Comparison of Productivity Growth, Journal of Political Economy 101 (193), 207-222

Cox, T.L., Chavas, J.P. 1990, A Nonparametric Analysis of Productivity: The Case of US Agriculture, European Review of Agricultural Economics 17 (1990), 449-464

Coxhead, I.A. 1992, Environment-Specific Rates and Biases of Technical Change in Agriculture, American Journal of Agricultural Economics 74 (1992), 592-604

Craig, B.J., Pardey, P.G. 1990, Multidimensional Output Indices, Department of Agricultural and Applied Economics, University of MN Staff Paper P 90-63

Craig, B.J., Pardey, P.G. 1990, Patterns of Agricultural Development in the United States, Department of Agricultural and Applied Economics, University of MN Staff Paper P 90-72

Craig, B.J., Pardey, P.G., Deininger, K.W. 1992, Capital in US Agriculture, University of Minnesota Staff Paper, forthcoming

Davis, J.S. 1979, Stability of the research production coefficient for US Agriculture, PhD Dissertation, University of Minnesota

Davis, J.S., Oram, P.A., Ryan, J.G. 1987, Assessment of Agricultural Research Priorities, An International Perspective, ACIAR Canberra

DeLong, J.B. 1988, Productivity Growth, Convergence, and Welfare: Comment, American Economic Review 78 (1988), 1138-54

Denison, E.F. 1969, Some Major Issues in Productivity Analysis: An Examination of Estimates by Jorgenson and Griliches, Survey of Current Business 49 (1969), 1-27

Dennison, E.F. 1972, Final Comments, Survey of Current Business 52 (1972), 95-110

Diewert, W.E. 1976, Exact and Superlative Index Numbers, Journal of Econometrics 4 (1976), 115-145

Dowrick, S., Nguyen, D. 1989, OECD Comparative Economic Growth 1950-85: Catch-up and Convergence, American Economic Review 79 (1989), 1010-1030

Englander, A.S. 1989, International Technology Transfer and Agricultural Productivity, in: Evenson, R.E., Pray, C.E. (Eds), Research and Productivity in Asian Agriculture, Cornell Ithaca

Evenson, R.E. 1988, Technological Opportunities and International Technology Transfer in Agriculture, in: Antonelli, C., Qadrio-Curzio, A. (Eds), The Agro-Technological System Towards 2000, North Holland Elsevier

Evenson, R.E. 1989, Spillover Benefits of Agricultural Research: Evidence from U.S. Experience, American Journal of Agricultural Economics 1989, 447-452

Evenson, R.E. 1991, Analyzing the Transfer of Agricultural Technology, Paper presented at Airlie House Conference 1991

Evenson, R.E., Kislev, Y. 1973, Research and Productivity in Wheat and Maize, Journal of Political Economy 1309-1329

Evenson, R.E., Landau, D., Ballou, D. 1987, Agricultural Productivity Measures for US States 1950-82, in: Evaluating Agricultural Research and Productivity, Symposium in Atlanta, GA

Evenson, R.E., Wagooner, P.E., Ruttan, V.W. 1979, Economic Benefits from Research: An Example from Agriculture, Science 205 (1979), 1001-1007

Evenson, R.E., Westphal, L. 1992, Technological Change and Technology Policies, Paper presented at First ADB Conference on Development Economics, Manila

Findlay, R., Kierzkowski, H. 1983, International Trade and Human Capital: A Simple General Equilibrium Model, Journal of Political Economy 91 (1983), 957-978

Frisvold, G.B. 1992, Induced Innovation and Longrun Factor Substitution: Implications for Research and Environmental Policy, Paper presented at AAEA meetings, Manhattan, KS

Garren, N.M., White, F.C. 1985, An Analysis of Agricultural Research Spillovers, Journal of Regional Studies 12 (1985), 25-36

Goto, A., Suzuki, k. 1989, R&D Capital, Rate of Return on R&D Investment and Spillover of R&D in Japanese Manufacturing Industries, Review of Economics and Statistics 71 (1989), 555-564

Griliches, Z. 1960, Measuring Inputs in Agriculture: A critical survey, Journal of Farm Economics 42 (1960), 1411-1427

Griliches, Z. 1960, The Demand for a Durable Input: US Farm Tractors, 1929-57, in: Harberger, A.C. (Ed.), The Demand for Durable Goods, Chicago, University of Chicago Press 181-207

Griliches, Z. 1979, Issues in Assessing the Contribution of R&D to Productivity Growth, Bell Journal of Economics 10 (1979), 92-116

Griliches, Z. 1980, R&D and Productivity Slowdown, American Economic Review 70 (1980), 343-348

Griliches, Z. 1986, Productivity, R&D, and Basic Research at the Firm Level in the 1970's, American Economic Review 76 (1086), 141-153

Griliches, Z. 1992, Sources of Agricultural Economic Growth and Productivity: Discussion, American Journal of Agricultural Economics 74 (1992), 762-63

Griliches, Z., Lichtenberg, F. 1984, Interindustry Technology Flows and Productivity Growth: A Reexamination, Review of Economics and Statistics 1984, 324-329

Grossman, G.M., Helpman, E. 1991, Innovation and Growth in the Global Economy, Cambridge, MA, MIT Press

Guttman, J.M. 1978, Interest Groups and the Demand for Agricultural Research, Journal of Political Economy 86 (1978), 467-483

Hatanaka, M, Wallace, T.D. 1980, Multicollinearity and the Estimation of Low-Order Moments in Stable Lag Distributions, in: kmenta, J., Ramsay, J. (Eds), Evaluation of Econometric Models, New York Academic Press

Hazilla, M., Kopp, R. 1986, Testing for Separable Functional Structure Using Partial Equilibrium Models, Journal of Econometrics 33 (1986), 119-142

Huffman, W.E., Evenson, R.E. 1989, Supply and Demand Functions for Multiproduct US Cash Grain Farms: Biases caused by Research and other Policies, American Journal of Agricultural Economics 71 (1989), 761-73

Huffman, W.E., Evenson, R.E. 1993, Science for Agriculture, Ames, Iowa State University Press

Huffman, W.E. 1978, Assessing Returns to Agricultural Extension, American Journal of Agricultural Economics 60 (1978), 59-79

Huffman, W.E., Miranowski, J.A. 1981, An Economic Analysis of Expenditures on Agricultural Experiment Station Research, American Journal of Agricultural Economics (1981), 104-118

Hulten, C.R. 1973, Divisia Index Numbers, Econometrica 41 (1973), 1017-25

Ibbotson Associates 1991, Stocks, Bonds, Bills, and Inflation, 1991 Yearbook, Chicago

Jaffee, A.B. 1986, Technological Opportunity and Spillovers of R&D: Evidence from Firms' Patents, Profits, and Market Value, American Economic Review 76 (1986), 984-1001

Jaffee, A.B. 1988, Demand and Supply Influences in R&D Intensity and Productivity Growth, Review of Economics and Statistics 1988, 431-437

Jaffee, A.B. 1989, Characterizing the "Technological Position" of Firms, with Application to Quantifying Technological Opportunity and Research Spillovers, Research Policy 18 (1989), 87-97

Jorgenson, D.W. 1966, The Embodiment Hypothesis, Journal of Political Economy 74 (1966), 1-14

Jorgenson, D.W. 1974, The Economic Theory of Replacement and Depreciation, in: Econometrics and Econometric Theory, Essays in Honor of Jan Tinbergen, IASP New York, 189-221

Jorgenson, D.W., Gollop, F.M, Fraumeni, B.M 1987, Productivity and US Economic Growth, Harvard University Press Cambridge, MA

Jorgenson, D.W., Griliches, Z. 1969, The Explanation of Productivity Change, Survey of Current Business 49 (1969), 31-64

Jorgenson, D.W., Gollop, F.M. 1992, Productivity Growth in US Agriculture: A Posterior Perspective, American Journal of Agricultural Economics 74 (1992), 745-750

Jorgenson, D.W., Griliches, Z. 1972, Issues in Growth Accounting: A Reply to Edward F. Dennison, Survey of Current Business 52 (1972), 65-94

Kawagoe, T., Hayami, Y. 1983, The Production Structure of World Agriculture: An Intercountry Cross-Section Analysis, The Developing Economies 21 (1983), 189-206

Kawagoe, T., Hayami, Y. 1985, An Intercountry Comparison of Agricultural Production Efficiency, American Journal of Agricultural Economics 67 (1985), 87-91

Kawagoe, T., Otsuka, Research., Hayami, Y. 1986, Induced Bias of Technical Change in Agriculture: The United States and Japan, 1880-1980, Journal of Political Economy 94 (1986), 523-544

King, R.G., Rebelo, S. 1990, Public Policy and Economic Growth: Developing Neoclassical Implications, Journal of Political Economy 98 (1990), S126-S150

Knutson, M., Tweeten, L.G. 1979, Toward an optimal rate of growth in agricultural production research and extension, American Journal of Agricultural Economics 61 (1979), 70-76

Lach, S., Schankerman, M. 1989, Dynamics of R&D and Investment in the Scientific Sector, Journal of Political Economy 97 (1989), 880-904

Latimer, R., Paarlberg, D. 1965, Geographic Distribution of Research Costs and Benefits, Journal of Farm Economics 47 (1965), 234-241

Lau, L.J. 1992, Aggregate Growth, Paper presented on first ADB Conference on Development Economics, Manila

Lau, L.J., Yotopolous, P.A. 1989, The Meta-Production Function Approach to Technological Change in World Agriculture, Journal of Development Economics 31 (1989), 241-269

Levin, R.C., Reiss, P.C. 1988, Cost-reducing and demand-creating R&D with Spillovers, Rand Journal of Economics 19 (1988), 538-556

Lichtenberg, F.R. 1987, The Effect of Government Funding on Private Industrial Research and Development: A Re-Assessment, Journal of Industrial Economics 36 (1987), 97-104

Lopez, R. 1980, The Structure of Production and the Derived Demand for Inputs in Canadian Agriculture, American Journal of Agricultural Economics 62 (1980), 38-45

Lopez, R. 1984, Estimating Substitution and Expansion Effects using a Cost Function Framework, American Journal of Agricultural Economics 66 (1984), 358-367

Martin, W., Alston, J.M. 1992, An Exact Approach for Evaluating the Benefits from Technological Change, World Bank Policy Research Working Paper WPS 1024, Washington

Mohnen, P.A., Nadiri, M.I., Prucha, I.R. 1986, R&D, Production Structure, and Rates of Return in the US, Japanese, and German Manufacturing Sectors, European Economic Review 30 (1986), 749-771

Murphy, K.M., Shleifer, A., Vishny, R.W. 1989, Industrialization and the Big Push, Journal of Political Economy 97 (1989), 1003-1026

Murphy, K.M., Shleifer, A., Vishny, R.W. 1993, Why is Rent Seeking so Costly to Growth? American Economic Review 83 (1993), 409-414

Norton, G.W., Davis, J.S. 1981, Evaluating Returns to Agricultural Research: A Review, American Journal of Agricultural Economics 63 (1982), 685-99

Olmstead, A.L., Rhode, P. 1993, Induced Innovation in American Agriculture: A Reconsideration, Journal of Political Economy 101 (1993), 100-118

Pardey, P.G., Eveleens, W., and Hallaway, M.L. forthcoming, A Statistical History of US Agricultural Research, CIFAP, St Paul, MN

Pardey, P.G. 1989, The Agricultural Knowledge Production Function: An empirical Look, Review of Economics and Statistics 71 (1989), 453-461

Pardey, P.G., Craig, B.J. 1989, Causal Relationships between Public Sector Agricultural Research Expenditures and Output, American Journal of Agricultural Economics 71 (1989), 9-19

Pardey, P.G., Craig, B.J., Hallaway, M.L. 1989, US Agricultural Research Deflators: 1890-1985, Research Policy 18 (1985), 289-296

Pasour, E.C., Johnson, M.A. 1982, Bureaucratic Productivity: The Case of Agricultural Research Revisited, Public Choice 37 (1982), 301-317

Peterson, W.L. 1976, A Note on the Social Returns to Private Research and Development, American Journal of Agricultural Economics 58 (1976), 324-326

Plant, M., Welch, F. 1984, Measuring the Impact of Education on Productivity, in: Dean, E. (Ed), Education and Economic Productivity, Ballinger Cambridge MA

Plucknett, D.L. Smith, N.J.H. 1986, Sustaining Agricultural Yields, Bioscience 36 (1986), 40-45

Rao, D.S.P., Sharma, K.C., Shepherd, W.F. 1991, On the Aggregation Problem in International Comparisons of Agricultural Production Aggregates, Journal of Development Economics 35 (1991), 197-204

Ray, S.C. 1982, A Translog Cost Function Analysis of U.S. Agriculture, 1939-77, American Journal of Agricultural Economics 1982, 490-498

Richter, M.K. 1966, Invariance Axioms and Economic Indexes, Econometrica 34 (1976), 739-55

Roe, T.L., Pardey, P.G. 1991, Economic Policy and Investment in Rural Public Goods; A Political Economy Perspective, in: Pardey, P.G., Roseboom, J., Anderson, J.R. (Eds) Agricultural Research Policy, Cambridge University Press

Romer, P.M. 1986, Increasing Returns and Long Run Growth, Journal of Political Economy 94 (1986), 1002-1038

Romer, P.M. 1987, Growth Based on Increasing Returns Due to Specialization, American Economic Review 77 (1987), 56-62

Rose-Ackerman, S., Evenson, R. 1985, The Political Economy of agricultural research and extension: Grants, Votes, and Reapportionment, American Journal of Agricultural Economics 1985, 1-14

Ruttan, V.W. 1987, Agricultural Research Policy and Development, FAO Research and Technology Paper 2, Rome

Schmitz, J.A. 1989, Imitation, Entrepreneurship, and Long Run Growth, Journal of Political Economy 97 (1989), 721-739

Schuh, G.E. 1976, The New Macroeconomics of Agriculture, American Journal of Agricultural Economics 58 (1976), 802-811

Schuh, G.E., Norton, G.W. 1991, Agricultural Research in an International Policy Context, in: Pardey, P.G., Roseboom, J., Anderson, J.R., Agricultural Resarch Policy, Cambridge University Press

Schultz, T.W. 1964, Transforming Traditional Agriculture, University of Chicago Press

Shumway, C.R. 1983, Supply, Demand and Technology in a Multiproduct Industry: Texas Field Crops, American Journal of Agricultural Economics 65 (1983), 748-760

Shumway, C.R. 1988, The Statistical Base for Agricultural Productivity Research: A Review and Critique, Chapter 4 in Capalbo and Antle (1988)

Thirtle, C.G. 1985, Induced Innovation in United States Field Crops 1939-1978, Journal of Agricultural Economics 36 (1985), 1-14

Triplett, J.E. 1983, Concepts of Quality in Input and Output Price Measures: A Resolution of the User-Value Resource-Cost Debate, in: Foss, M.F. (Ed.), The US National Income and Product Accounts: Selected Topics, University of Chicago Press, 269-311

Trueblood, M.A., Ruttan, V.W. 1992, A Comparison of Multifactor Productivity Calculations of the US Agricultural Sector, University of MN, mimeo

Umali, D.L. 1992, Public and Private Sector Roles in Agricultural Research. Theory and Experience, World Bank Discussion Paper 176, Washington DC

Villezca-Becerra, P.A., Shumway, C.R. 1992, State-Level Output Supply and Input Demand Elasticities for Agricultural Commodities, Journal of Agricultural Economics and Research 44 (1992), 22-34

White, F.C., Havliceck 1982, Optimal expenditures for agricultural research and extension: Implications of Underfunding, American Journal of Agricultural Economics 64 (1982), 47-55

Yee, J. 1992, Assessing Rates of Return to Public and Private Agricultural Research, Journal of Agricultural Economics and Research 44 (1992), 35-41

INDEX

For Product Safety Concerns and Information please contact our EU
representative GPSR@taylorandfrancis.com
Taylor & Francis Verlag GmbH, Kaufingerstraße 24, 80331 München, Germany

9 780367 254681